Praise for *Finding*

"To understand and be [...] [...] [...] ir marriages is a game-changer. The power to create [...] [...] [...] er to build up, the power to help our husbands become the men that God created them to be—what a gift! This book will cause you to look at your marriage through a new lens. You will love better, trust better, pray better, and encourage better because of this book. Thank you, Juli, for this gift to marriages around the world!"

—**Jamie Ivey,** bestselling author and host of
The Happy Hour with Jamie Ivey podcast

"In truth, I cannot say enough about the beauty, power, and potency of this book. These words found me at the exact moment of need in my own marriage, and I found myself wanting to highlight line after line as simple yet profound truths were so clearly articulated. Juli has done a masterful job of weaving together personal narrative, biblical exposition, practical teaching, and prophetic illumination of God's heart and divine design of man, woman, and the mystery of marriage. These pages held keys to understanding the 'whys' behind some of my own angsts, and helped me tangibly grasp some of the inner wirings of my husband's complex and powerful design. I am so grateful to have this resource and am grateful for Juli's revisitation to this timeless impartation and exhortation. I wholeheartedly encourage every woman to dive into the depths of this work, willfully inviting the Holy Spirit to minister to your heart where and how He intends. I am walking away humbled, encouraged, equipped and impassioned to continue investing intentionally into my marriage for the glory of God!"

—**Mo (Isom) Aiken,** *New York Times* bestselling author of *Wreck My Life: Journeying from Broken to Bold, Sex, Jesus and the Conversations the Church Forgot,* and *Fully Known: An Invitation to True Intimacy with God*

"I've been married over forty years, and I have read a lot of books on being a wife. *Finding the Hero in Your Husband* is a must read! I wish I had this book when I was younger. It would have saved me from making many mistakes that caused a lot of pain. Read it now! You will be glad you did, and your husband will thank you for decades to come."

—**Ann Wilson,** co-host of the *Family Life Today* radio broadcast and co-author of *Vertical Marriage*

"In this empowering book, *Finding the Hero in Your Husband,* Juli Slattery is helping us take our eyes off the imperfections of our spouse, ourselves, and our marriage, and put them onto Christ, the only truly perfect Hero. I love how she unpacks common issues we all face as wives by helping us look a little deeper to see what's happening underneath the surface of our hearts and marriage. *Finding the Hero in Your Husband* helps us to practically identify, navigate and heal from the disappointments, disillusionments, and distortions that may be keeping us stuck so that we can discover the beautiful revelation of God's heart that He intended us to experience through marriage."

—**Francie Winslow,** wife, mom of six, host of *Heaven in Your Home* podcast

finding
the hero

revisited

finding the hero

in your husband

embracing your
power in marriage

dr. juli slattery

foreword by jackie hill perry

Health Communications, Inc.
Boca Raton, Florida
www.hcibooks.com

Library of Congress Cataloging-in-Publication Data

Names: Slattery, Julianna, 1969- author.

Title: Finding the hero in your husband, revisited : embracing your power
in marriage / Dr. Juli Slattery.

Other titles: Finding the hero in your husband

Description: Boca Raton : Health Communications, Inc., 2021. | Revision of
Finding the hero in your husband.

Identifiers: LCCN 2021020481 | ISBN 9780757323928 (paperback) | ISBN
9780757323935 (ePub) | ISBN 0757323928 (paperback) | ISBN 0757323936
(ePub)

Subjects: LCSH: Wives—Religious life. | Christian women—Religious life.

Classification: LCC BV4528.15 .S53 2021 | DDC 248.8/435—dc23

LC record available at https://lccn.loc.gov/2021020481

ISBN-13: 978-0-7573-2392-8 (Paperback)
ISBN-10: 07573-2392-8 (Paperback)
ISBN-13: 978-0-7573-2393-5 (ePub)
ISBN-10: 07573-2393-6 (ePub)

Publisher: Health Communications, Inc.
        1700 NW 2nd Avenue
        Boca Raton, FL 33432-1653

Cover design by Hannah Nitz
Interior design by Larissa Hise Henoch, formatting by Lawna Patterson Oldfield

To my Swoo
You are THAT Hero!

contents

foreword

The hardest relationship I have ever known is the one I have with my husband. In the beginning, I didn't know it would be that way. A steady diet of Disney movies and rom coms (as Juli discusses in a later chapter) discipled me, in a way. The lonely princess finds the man with the chiseled jaw and bright eyes. They meet, then marry, and forever after they are happy—supposedly, that is. My romanticized idealism faded quickly. An argument here, boxer shorts left on the floor there, silent treatment and forced make up sex; the tale of real life. When we struggled over anything, it was easy to lift my hand and extend a finger his way. When two sinners turned saints say "I do," we bring our sin patterns with us; therefore, there is always the possibility that someone is legitimately guilty. At some point, I learned how boring blame is. Boring because it only works to identify a problem through shaming, and when has shame ever brought anyone to repentance? After every pointed finger, harsh tone, and desire to quit, I had to realize that I may not be able to change who I married, but I do have the power to change who he is married to: me.

The hard things in my relationship with my husband are a mirror. If and when I choose to look, I'll discover myself. It's interesting that

I not only had an imaginary framework for marriage, but the lens by which I viewed myself was also a fantasy. Thus, the tendency to blame was commonplace because, clearly, my husband was the problem, not my ego. But what if in all of the difficulty of marriage, God wanted me to see where I am weak, where I am unbelieving, where I am immature, so that as I seek the Father, Son, and Holy Spirit, I not only become a better wife but a better Christian? As Juli rightly posits, "Rather than sabotaging intimacy, what if those lonely nights and crushed expectations are part of the journey of crossing that shaky bridge to a deeper experience of love?" I can only find the hero in my husband once I have the humility of mind and distinguished character to do so. From there, what I become for my husband is less of an adversary and more of a lover, supporter, and friend. There's a world of vulnerability in loving like this, but remember Jesus who loved us the same.

I said all of this to prepare you for what's coming. As is expected of someone with Juli's experience, her words are informative, insightful, and just plain ol' wise. As I read this book, I saw myself in a new light. My fears and pride were exposed, but there was no shame in sight, only hope. Just as the possibilities for what our husbands can be with our and the Holy Spirit's help are endless, the same is true of us. The hard parts of our marriages don't tell the whole story, and the weakest parts of you are not all you are. There is so much more love, joy, and intimacy to be discovered and that is good news, so, as Juli closes, so will I: "When those who know me best reflect on my life, let them not say, 'She was a happy wife,' but 'She was a faithful woman.' May the same be said of you!"

And to that I say, "Amen."

—Jackie Hill Perry

acknowledgments

To you, the reader. Stating the obvious, without you I wouldn't have written this book. I imagined your face and prayed for you as I wrote. Thank you for your grace as you read, remembering that I'm just one woman wanting to encourage another.

I want to say thank you to the four men in my life. Mike, thank you for putting up with me as I went into my writing submarine and for always being my sounding board. You've written this book with me over the twenty-seven years of our marriage. Every year grows sweeter! Michael, Andrew, and Christian, I know it's not always easy to have a mom who writes books on relationships, marriage, and sex. You are all three so encouraging to me. I look forward to watching how the Lord develops the "hero" in each of you. You are amazing young men!

Mom and Dad, you have lived out the message of this book for over sixty years, and I had a front-row seat. In some ways, I just wrote what I saw. Thank you for your example of love and faithfulness and for all the ways you have encouraged and equipped me over the years.

To the Authentic Intimacy team, each one of you contributed to this project in different ways. Kristi, you were my first line of editing. Suzanne, you managed the ministry so I could focus on writing. Joy, you set up pilot study groups for me to get feedback. Jacci and Hope, you've helped me with promotions and marketing. I couldn't do it without you! Many thanks to the Authentic Intimacy board members for your support, prayer, and encouragement. Special thanks to Janae Payton and Linda Dillow, who gave me valuable feedback.

Anna and Keith, you have been so generous in sharing your beautiful Lake House with us so I could get away and write.

Hannah, the way the cover for this book came about will always make me giggle. I love that your enthusiasm and creativity show up as the face of this book!

To my 6 AM group: Rachel, Havi, and Julie. I've loved watching God work in your marriages. Thank you to the other women who went through the pilot studies of this book: Maritza, Brooke, Ashlei, Julie, Krista, Bethany, Keyla, Shelli, Becca, Miranda, Evelyn, Melanie, Courtney, Debbie, Linda, Vilmarie, Allison, Kelly, and CJ. You ladies were so vulnerable as you processed the message of this book! Sue Bracefield, thank you for your input from the other side of the world.

Robert and Andrew Wolgemuth, thank you for your help and wisdom in getting this project off the ground.

Finally, to the HCI team. You believed in this book twenty years ago and you are still investing in it. Thank you, Christine Belleris, for your work with me on editing. Thank you, Christian Blonshine, vice president; Larissa Hise Henoch, art director; Lori Golden, sales; Lindsey Mach, public relations director; Lori Lewis and Anthony Clausi, proofreaders; and Friederich Schulte, copyeditor.

author's note

You may not know this, but I wrote a first version of this book in 1999. A lot has changed! I had only been married for five years and was in the trenches of trying to figure out how to make my marriage work. The wrinkles on my face indicate that I'm no longer that young woman.

I also wrote the first book when I was very new in ministry. Over the years, my counseling career transitioned into becoming a teacher and eventually a Christian voice on marriage issues, particularly intimacy. These years of personal and professional experience have challenged and seasoned the nuggets of wisdom I had stumbled on so long ago. I'm no longer just that girlfriend writing from the perspective of trying to figure things out. I now have the confidence that this stuff actually works!

My personal life has evolved over twenty years, but so has the world in which we are living. In 1999 there were no smart phones, and the Internet was a relatively new invention. Technology has revolutionized how we learn, communicate, and spend our free time. We have also seen dramatic shifts in the ways men and women interact. Women have become increasingly empowered, outpacing men in obtaining advanced degrees and highly respected careers like law and medicine. The #metoo movement has given voice to women who have been exploited, devalued, and abused within both secular and Christian environments.

The Western world has become progressively postmodern and post-Christian in our approach to the meaning of life, morality, and the pursuit of fulfillment. This worldview shift has had huge implications for how we understand and approach marriage. Take sex, for example, it's no longer considered primarily for "making babies" or even to be reserved for marriage. Sex has become a vehicle for personal expression and fulfillment. Even gender is now up for debate. A lot of people will reject the underlying foundation of this book that men and women are fundamentally different.

As I read through the "old" version of *Finding the Hero in Your Husband*, I recognized that many of the examples and nuances from back then would not connect with today's Christian woman. But I also realized that the book contained nuggets of wisdom that I had learned as a young wife, and I longed to pass down these truths to my spiritual "daughters." What you will find in these pages is a massive rewrite of the principles that have guided me through twenty-seven years of marriage (and counting). God's Word hasn't changed, but applying it to different cultures and time frames is an ongoing challenge.

I will share with you up front that I believe God created marriage for a purpose. I believe that His Word contains ageless wisdom to guide us through the challenges of modern-day marriages. This means that much of what I've written in this book may conflict with the larger cultural definitions of love, intimacy, and marriage itself. Don't say I didn't warn you. But remember that the world's "wisdom" is considered foolishness to God and vice versa. Being a follower of Jesus Christ means that we see everything, including marriage, through a different lens.

Why This Book Is for You

If you and I had met for coffee every week for the past twenty-seven years, this book contains much of what I would love to have shared with you. I've written about how you as a wife can partner with God in the redemptive process of your marriage.

Do you know that you have a lot of power in your marriage? Your power is a dynamic tool that can be used either to build intimacy or to sabotage it. Most likely, you don't understand the power God has given you, so you don't know how to use it to build intimacy.

I'm guessing you've been working hard to improve your relationship with your husband. Women know how to work hard. Yet, effort does not always mean working wisely. There have been many seasons in which I've worked hard at marriage, but my work did little to impact intimacy. Sometimes, my efforts did damage to my marriage. I made a lot of mistakes because I didn't understand my power. I'm guessing that you will be able to personally relate to this struggle in your own marriage.

This is not a "husband-improvement project." I'm not promising you that if you "follow these simple steps, your marriage will instantly improve." The reason you will read this book is that you sincerely want to know how to honor the Lord in your marriage, or are at least curious to know what that means.

This book will focus exclusively on your role within your marriage. I get it—your husband has definitely contributed his share of mess to your relationship. It probably wouldn't take you long to point out how your husband has let you down. But here's the thing: You will never improve your marriage by focusing on what he is doing wrong. Your greatest task is understanding how you should respond to the unique challenges within your marriage.

While this book doesn't come with a "money-back guarantee," I am sharing time-tested principles with you that will greatly improve your chances of a thriving relationship with your husband. Please remember that you are only accountable and responsible for how you steward your power in your marriage. If you want to understand the power God has given you and how to use it in a way that honors Him and promotes intimacy, this book is for you. My prayer is that God has put this resource in your hands as a vehicle for practical changes in your marriage but also to draw you deeper into a personal relationship with God Himself.

Chapter 1

disappointment:
the end or beginning
of intimacy?

"Should I marry him?"

As a twenty-three-year-old woman, I couldn't decide if Mike was *the one*. I had friends who fell madly in love and others who just knew a guy was her soul mate. The decision to get married was less obvious for me. Mike and I had talked about marriage, and I struggled with whether or not we were right for each other.

For months, I approached my friends and family members with an invisible clipboard, polling them on their opinion. "What should I do? Do you think we're a good match?" My mom summed up what everyone else said, "Juli, I would never tell you who to marry. That's such a huge decision that I would never want that responsibility. You have to pray about it and decide for yourself." I had dated Mike on and off for a few years. We had fun together, and he made me feel safe. Yes, I was attracted to him, but marriage? We came from such different backgrounds! How could it ever work? I wished God would just tell me what to do.

As a psychologist in training, I knew how quickly "happily ever after" could sour into misery. Even as a young woman, I had witnessed my share of marital train wrecks. My clinical training made me paranoid to make a commitment with so many unknowns and my perceived lifelong happiness on the line. Every week, I met with women who regretted getting married. I heard about affairs, emotional abuse, and people simply "falling out of love." If I wasn't 100 percent sure that Mike was, indeed, the one, should I still commit my life to this man?

Even the night before our wedding, I told the Lord, "If you want to stop this marriage, I'm okay with that." One morning on our honeymoon, I woke up with my husband beside me and felt nothing short of panic. *What did I just do? This is forever!*

In truth, easy, blissful marriages are the absolute exception (if they exist at all). A few decades later, my friends who had experienced love at first sight have shared with me their own stories of disappointments. Some of those friends are no longer married to their soul mates. It turns out being certain that you found the one doesn't save you from heartache and potentially divorce.

As the days, weeks, months, and years of marriage pile up, so do unresolved conflicts, frustrations, and difficult life circumstances. There's just no getting around it. The forging of two people into one union is a mysterious and painful journey.

Marriage has been described as "a romance in which the hero dies in the first chapter." It usually doesn't take long to hit a wall in marriage...a wall that prompts you to wonder, *Would this have been easier if I had married someone else?* You didn't sign up for life with a man who complains about his job, is addicted to video games, or goes through months of depression. Hitting this wall of disillusionment may make you want to give up on the idea of marriage altogether. More people are choosing to cohabit rather than marry, not because they don't want a happy marriage but because they don't believe it's attainable.[i]

A lot of women rightly ask, "Why sign up for such a potential of heartbreak and frustration?" Marriage offers the greatest chance at intimacy here on planet Earth. By intimacy, I don't mean sex; I'm referring to what the best sex symbolizes. The beauty of being naked, embraced, and united. Intimacy is when the shaky bridge between two people is miraculously traversed. With all its pitfalls and pain points, no human relationship more powerfully speaks to our longings to be known, loved, and accepted.

The Greatest Obstacle to Intimacy

Have you ever considered that true intimacy may actually require seasons of disappointment? Rather than sabotaging intimacy, what if those lonely nights and crushed expectations are part of the journey of crossing that shaky bridge to a deeper experience of love?

When our children were little, we took them to the magical land of Walt Disney World, the "happiest place on earth." At Cinderella's castle, we ate breakfast with many of the Disney characters. Among them were Cinderella and her handsome Prince Charming. When the fairy-tale couple got to our table, I playfully asked them about their marriage. Prince Charming looked lovingly into his bride's eyes, held her hands, and said, "We have been married for over fifty years and are still madly in love." I asked, "What is your secret?" "Living in Walt Disney World!" the Prince replied. Of course! Cinderella and Prince Charming are frozen in time. They have not aged or faced the realities of life. For many decades, they have lived in the blissful bubble of their wedding day. In fact, they still wear the same costumes.

On the surface, their fairy-tale marriage seems to represent the starry-eyed love we all hope to preserve in marriage. We want the butterflies and optimism of new love. But new love is not the same thing as intimacy. In fact, those feelings of love have to fade in order for us to develop the mature love that marriage is really all about.

Those feelings of love have to fade in order for us to develop the mature love that marriage is really all about.

Bethany shared with me, "I've definitely seen the Disney lie in my own life—and a lot of my pain as a young bride came from the fact that I felt like I was robbed of the Disney World experience. We didn't have much of a honeymoon, and we lived with his parents after our wedding. Add some health issues, a sixty-hour workweek for my husband, and an hour long commute each way, and we didn't really get the newlywed experience I wanted. During the hard times in our engagement, when all I wanted was to push sexual limits, I held on to the idea that once we got married everything would be easy, breezy, and beautiful. But the picture on the box didn't match what I found inside, and it was devastating. It took a long time for me to work through that disappointment and embrace the idea that true intimacy was born and nurtured in life's difficulties."

What if our understanding of love and marriage is the problem? Think about much of the entertainment marketed for women, both young and old. Movies, Netflix series, and romance novels consistently tell us a story of a woman searching for intimacy. After trying love with a few losers, finally she stumbles upon Mr. Right. After the agonizing tension of, "Will they ever get together?"

the story ends when the two of them overcome some barrier and realize that they really are in love. The message is clear: Find the prince and you will become a princess. His love will rescue you. You just have to attract the right one, and then you will live happily ever after. The stretches of marriage that feel unfulfilling in real life can immediately make you wonder, *Is marriage so difficult because I married the wrong guy?*

A Duke University ethics professor, Stanley Hauerwas, put it this way, "We always marry the wrong person. We never know whom we marry; we just think we do. Or even if we first marry the right person, just give it a little while and he or she will change."[ii]

I remember one young wife, Jess, who was ready to walk away from her marriage three years into it. During their engagement, she developed an attraction to her fiancé's best friend. Just a few weeks before the wedding, Jess ended up in bed with him. They promised never to do it again and to never speak of it. With all the pressure of a wedding, Jess buried the secret and got married. Every disagreement and every annoying habit of her new husband became a trigger to wonder, *How would life have been better if I had married his best friend instead?* By the time she met me for counseling, Jess had convinced herself that God had always wanted her to marry the other guy and that her current marriage really was a mistake.

The expectations of what love should feel like can play tricks on us. Some women, like Jess, deal with this disappointment and confusion by trading husbands. Many more live on with broken dreams and guarded hearts.

The question is not whether or not you will be disappointed in marriage, but rather what you will do with the disappointment that inevitably occurs.

God's plan is that a wedding displays love in its infancy, not its maturity. Intimacy can only grow and develop over a lifetime of living together within the safety of a commit-

The very nature of intimacy requires that the illusion of being *in love* is replaced with the choice *to love*.

ted love. Working through conflicts, accepting differences, weathering storms, admitting selfishness, and anger are all necessary difficulties that allow genuine love to grow. Unfortunately, many couples believe that such disappointments signal the end of intimacy instead of the beginning. *But the fairy tale must end for the potential of true intimacy to begin.*

You see, we don't know what love is until it no longer comes naturally. The very nature of intimacy requires that the illusion of being *in love* is replaced with the choice *to love*.

Believing Through Disappointment

Many years ago, I had the opportunity to interview Dr. Scott Stanley, who is a renowned marriage researcher. He made a statement based on his research that has stuck with me: Your greatest chance of happiness is the marriage you are currently in. Yes, some marriages are toxic and destructive. But the great majority of difficult marriages are two people who have gotten stuck somewhere on the road to intimacy.

God has designed the mystery of intimacy to be achieved through two very imperfect humans. Couples exchanging their wedding vows are ordinary men and women who have weaknesses, vulnerabilities, and insecurities—no matter how much they may wish to hide these inadequacies from each other. Both of them will soon learn the inevitability of disappointment. It is only through the acceptance of each other's faults that the love they hope for can begin to become a reality. This is the central idea that I hope to share with you in this book: A woman never marries the man of her dreams. She helps the man she marries to become the man of his dreams.

Tori had hit the wall at year eight in her marriage. She had mustered the strength to believe and hope for the best in Andrew until she no longer did. She was just tired of carrying the weight of his irresponsibility. He had changed jobs three times in the last four years while she balanced a demanding schedule as a nurse while also carrying the bulk of care for their two young children. Over the years, asking turned to pleading, and pleading had turned to indifference. Why even try? It was useless. He was useless.

A woman never marries the man of her dreams. She helps the man she marries to become the man of his dreams.

As Tori's frustration grew, she had built walls around her heart to protect her from continual disappointment. Long gone were the days when being with Andrew meant fun and laughter. Honestly, their relationship had begun to resemble more of a critical mom and a lazy son. What's romantic about that?

Before the wedding, a woman, like Tori, sees a bright hope in her fiancé. She may see glimpses of his sensitivity, his strength, and his commitment. After the wedding, she only sees his weaknesses. Her disappointment may initially feel like a crushing blow. It becomes painfully obvious to her that he cannot meet all her needs. Now she has a choice: to respond in anger to his weakness or to invest with faith in his strength. For intimacy to grow, she must believe in his potential. She can invest in the real-life hero that lies hidden beneath his doubts and insecurities.

The secret of intimacy in marriage is not finding a hero *to be* your husband but finding the hero *in* your husband. God has given every woman the power to help her husband grow, over time, into the godly man that he can become. Unfortunately, many women are so devastated by what he *is not* today that they refuse to invest

The secret of intimacy in marriage is not finding a hero *to be* your husband but finding the hero *in* your husband.

in the man he *could become* tomorrow. This is not about feeding your fantasy of changing your husband into the perfect man. It's about expanding your vision and expectation for the work God wants to do, first in your own life, and then in his.

What a Real Hero Looks Like

"Finding the *hero* in your husband." What does that mean? There is a lot of talk today about what makes a hero. How does one become a hero? Through special talents or athletic prowess? Superhuman feats? Daring rescues? If these are the criteria, where is the "hero" in the average husband?

The essence of heroics is the consistent choice to sacrifice for others. War heroes put their lives on the line for a military cause. Police officers and firefighters willingly place themselves in harm's way to protect others. Unsung heroes give up their own glory or desires in order to allow others to flourish.

Your husband has been created and called to emulate the greatest of heroes, Jesus Christ.

The Bible indicates that your human, earthly marriage is about more than you and your husband. The covenant of marriage was created by God to be a tangible, practical way that human beings experience an echo of God's love for His chosen people. I know that is a big concept to grasp, but don't skip past it.

Marriage is so holy, so difficult, and so important because it is an earthly picture of God's passionate and faithful love. Ephesians

5 says this most clearly. The apostle Paul is teaching on marriage in this passage. Essentially, he is saying that marriage is like a jigsaw puzzle (yes, this is my interpretation!). A husband and wife can't put the pieces of the puzzle together until they know what's on the front of the box...the picture the pieces are designed to create. Look at Ephesians 5:21–33 in this light:

Submit to one another out of reverence for Christ.

Wives, submit yourselves to your own husbands as you do to the Lord. For the husband is the head of the wife as Christ is the head of the church, his body, of which he is the Savior. Now as the church submits to Christ, so also wives should submit to their husbands in everything.

Husbands, love your wives, just as Christ loved the church and gave himself up for her to make her holy, cleansing her by the washing with water through the word, and to present her to himself as a radiant church, without stain or wrinkle or any other blemish, but holy and blameless. In this same way, husbands ought to love their wives as their own bodies. He who loves his wife loves himself. After all, no one ever hated their own body, but they feed and care for their body, just as Christ does the church—for we are members of his body. "For this reason a man will leave his father and mother and be united to his wife, and the two will become one flesh." This is a profound mystery—but I am talking about Christ and the church. However, each one of you also must love his wife as he loves himself, and the wife must respect her husband. (Eph. 5:21–33 NIV)

In later chapters, we will come back to this passage. And yes, we will deal with the submission word. But for right now, I want you to see that the *reason* for marriage is that it is a profound mystery that is meant to be an echo of Christ and the church.

This "puzzle" of marriage has a hero in the picture. Your husband has been cast in the role of a lover who denies himself for the sake of his beloved. Jesus Christ is the ultimate hero. Not only did he give his life on the cross, but he spent his days on Earth sacrificially ministering to the needs of others. This is exactly the role to which God has called every husband. He is to give himself to his wife, just as Christ gave Himself for the church.

In your heart, this is the hero you are looking for . . . and honestly, this is the hero your husband also longs to become. No wonder you're disappointed in your husband! And no wonder he shies away from such an impossible task! You were made to be "married to Jesus."

There are three important things that you need to keep in mind as you work through this book.

1. HEROES ARE FORMED, NOT BORN.

Sorry to disappoint you, but husband heroes are never found in young men with larger-than-life dreams and six-pack abs. Yes, some men, even at a young age are honorable and caring, but becoming a hero is a process of maturity.

I think of my friend Esther, who met her husband, Pete, at Bible college. Before they met, they both had devoted their lives to God. Esther saw Pete's integrity, dedication, and passion for God even when he was twenty years old. But eleven years and four children into their marriage, Esther called me in tears. Pete had just told her about a six-month affair with a coworker. How could a godly husband do such a cruel thing to his wife and family? Walking toward integrity is not a "one and done" decision. Even if you are married to a godly, loving husband, he still battles sin, selfishness, and fear.

God uses failure, trials, and disappointments to chip away at ambitions and fears to forge in a man the heroics he is called to embody. Stories of heroic husbands are almost invariably stories of seasoned men and their seasoned wives who, often through great challenges, have learned the secret of surrender.

Robertson McQuilkin's life represents the type of hero that every woman longs to discover in her husband. After forty years of marriage, his wife Muriel fell prey to Alzheimer's. At the time, Robertson was the president of Columbia International University. As Muriel's health faded, Robertson was faced with the choice of either putting her in a memory-care facility or retiring from his position to care for her full-time. Here are his words about his decision:

> As she needed more and more of me, I wrestled daily with the question of who gets me full time—Muriel or Columbia Bible College and Seminary. When the time came, the decision was firm. It took no great calculation. It was a matter of integrity. Had I not promised, forty-two years before, "in sickness and in health till death do us part?" This was no grim duty to which I was stoically resigned, however. It was only fair. She had, after all, cared for me for almost four decades with marvelous devotion; now it was my turn. Such a partner she was!

> If I took care of her for forty years, I would never be out of her debt. She is such a delight to me. I don't have to care for her, I get to.

> I have been startled by the response to the announcement of my resignation. Husbands and wives renew marriage vows, pastors tell the story to their congregations. It was a mystery to me until a distinguished oncologist, who lives

constantly with dying people, told me, "Almost all women stand by their men; very few men stand by their women." Perhaps people sensed this contemporary tragedy and, somehow, were helped by a simple choice I considered to be my only option.

It is all more than keeping promises and being fair, however. As I watch her brave descent into oblivion, Muriel is the joy of my life. Daily, I discern new manifestations of the kind of person she is, the wife I always loved. I also see fresh manifestations of God's love—the God I long to love more fully.[iii]

Robertson McQuilkin became a hero. He was not a perfect man, but in the latter years of his marriage, he had learned the secret joy of laying down his life for his beloved. Yet I wish we had journals from Robertson and Muriel during the early years of their marriage. Without a doubt, young Muriel had days and even seasons in which she thought of her ambitious husband as insensitive and unloving. Did this hero, Robertson, ever leave his dirty laundry on the floor, choose his work over his wife, or yell at their children? I wonder what choices this young woman made in those moments to become the wife her husband described: *"Muriel is the joy of my life. Daily, I discern new manifestations of the kind of person she is, the wife I always loved."*

Havi's husband, Anthony, after three years of marriage described becoming a hero this way:

Every hero story sees a metamorphosis where the character becomes the hero as he sheds his boy-like tendencies and becomes a man. This process is always done in the face of adversity, where in the trial, the hero rejects the comfort of a boy-like cowardice and embraces deep responsibilities.

The hero's shift goes from inward-focused selfishness to out-ward focusing, caring about others (most particularly the heroine). Something switches in you when you are face to face with failure, and still, someone believes in you. When they believe that you have what it takes to rise above the pain, persevere, and not quit. That is what changes a boy into a man and calls forth the hero within.

You may not see right now the impact you have on your husband's life, but the everyday choices of how you interact shape who he is becoming. As a wife, you have God-given influence to either bring out the hero or to bury it deeper within your husband's fear and insecurity.

2. GOD IS MORE CONCERNED WITH YOUR CHARACTER THAN WITH YOUR ROMANCE.

Your marriage is important to God, but there is something infinitely more priceless to Him: your faith. Peter told the early Christians that their faith was more precious than gold.[iv] Just as gold is refined by fire, our faith is tested and strengthened by trials.

When God gives you seasons of romance, love, and fulfillment, thank Him. But when marriage is disappointing and lonely, He is in the midst of that season, too.

As a young woman polling my family and friends about whether or not I should marry Mike, I couldn't have perceived the ways God would bless me through marriage...not because I married the right guy, but because I determined to be the right woman. I'm thankful not primarily for the ways my husband has changed over the years, but for how God has changed me. God has never wasted a moment of pain in my life. He is refining me through the very problems I wished I would never have to face.

3. YOUR HUSBAND WILL NEVER FULFILL YOU.

An intimate marriage gives us an echo or picture of God's love, but you were made for more than even the greatest of those echoes. Finding the hero is not about depending on your husband for fulfillment. Ironically, it is only through letting go of the hope of your husband's perfect love that you will be free to invest in true intimacy. That hero in your husband is only his capacity to reflect to you God's loving kindness, mercy, and grace.

In many marriages, a husband takes great steps to becoming the sacrificial hero he is called to be. But even so, he is human. Ultimately, he is only able to be a shadow of the true hero we all long for. He needs a hero greater than himself. A hero who gives strength to the weary, courage to the fearful, and guidance to the bewildered. Marriage is a delicate balance of believing in the emerging "husband hero" only because our trust is foundationally placed in the true hero.

God wants you to embrace Him as the ultimate romance of your life, not just the means to a happy marriage.

As we walk through this book together, I will be referring back and forth between building your marriage and learning to trust God. Finding the hero in your husband is a lifelong process, one in which you will have both moments of despair and seasons of hope. You cannot force your husband to love you, nor can you alone make your marriage an intimate one. You can only do your part. To sustain you, you need a bigger goal than a happy marriage and a greater god than romance. Right now, you may want a relationship with God so He will help you build a great marriage. That's a wonderful place to start! But eventually, God wants you to embrace Him as the ultimate romance of your life, not just the means to a happy marriage.

One of my life verses is Proverbs 14:1: "The wise woman builds her house, but with her own hands the foolish one tears hers down." Are you ready to start building together?

Endnotes

i   https://www.theatlantic.com/health/archive/2012/02/the-marriage-problem-why-many-are-choosing-cohabitation-instead/252505/.

ii Stanley Hauerwas, "Sex and Politics: Bertrand Russell and 'Human Sexuality,'" *Christian Century*, April 19, 1978, 417–422. Also found online at https://zschlegel.wordpress.com/2014/02/11/we-always-marry-the-wrong-person-stanley-hauerwas/.

iii Robertson McQuilkin, "Living by Vows," *Christianity Today's Marriage Partnership*, Fall 1996.

iv I Peter 1:7.

Chapter 2

power for a purpose

As the mom of three sons, I've spent my share of time on the floor surrounded by Legos. For many years, Christmas morning consisted of helping my boys build spaceships, castles, and race cars. As the boys got older, the projects became more complicated.

Nothing was more frustrating than realizing that somewhere in the building process, we got a piece wrong. To move forward, we had to carefully deconstruct the Legos to correct whatever mistake distorted the model.

My marriage has sometimes felt this way. One day we are clipping along with life and then, BOOM. We are in conflict. We have a problem that seems to keep us from moving forward. Sometimes the problem can be resolved with communication and grace, but other times, it reveals something wrong with the "model" of our marriage. Somewhere along the way, we got a piece wrong in the foundation. If we just try to muscle through the problem, something about the structure of our marriage will be skewed no matter how much we try to communicate through it.

Moving forward in intimacy often requires some "deconstruction" to figure out what's gone wrong in the building process. You and your husband have established patterns of relating, some healthy and others…not so much. In this chapter, we will tear apart some Legos of your marriage, examining the principle of relational power. Proverbs 14:1 refers to a wise woman either building or tearing down her home. The building or destruction is all about how a wife uses her power. The key to finding the hero in your husband is learning to use your power well.

Let me warn you, this chapter is going to feel like work. You might even bristle as we explore your husband's needs. We aren't going to stay here for long, but this information is foundational to understanding why you may feel like you are running in circles as you try to fix your marriage. You will learn in this chapter that your husband's needs translate into your power. Understanding your power is the key to how you can impact your marriage. So, roll up your sleeves and hang in there as we dive in!

Understanding Relational Power

Have you ever paid too much for something because you were in desperate need? I've shelled out $25 for a simple salad because I needed food and there were few healthy options available. There have been times when I'd have gladly paid exorbitantly for something to distract my screaming children. We go to an emergency room with no idea of how huge that bill will be because someone we love needs immediate medical attention. When the need is great, we willingly surrender to the terms of one who can meet it.

This principle applies to relationships. When you need something from someone, that gives a person power. Husbands and wives, by God's design, trust each other (in some areas, exclusively) for many of their emotional needs to be met. This means that both you and your husband have a lot of power.

Building an intimate marriage is all about how we use our relational power. When marriage goes wrong, both a husband and wife use their power to keep themselves safe rather than to create a safe environment. As we look at the Legos (or building blocks) of your marriage, we need to begin with understanding your relational power.

In the next chapter, we will look at how your needs as a woman give your husband power. For now, let's look at your husband's core needs, which naturally translate into your power.

When marriage goes wrong, both a husband and wife use their power to keep themselves safe rather than to create a safe environment.

Need #1: Your Husband Needs Respect

If you've read Christian books on marriage or have ever been to a marriage conference, a husband's need for respect is not a new concept for you. In fact, you've probably heard about men and respect so many times that you're tempted to breeze right past this section. Many years ago, that would have been my reaction. *Yes, the Bible says that wives should respect their husbands. Got that. Let's move on.*

Not so fast. While most women have heard that respect is a big deal for men, they likely don't know why it's so critical to intimacy. Respecting your husband is about more than following some archaic biblical teaching. It's recognizing that the intimacy of marriage exposes your man to the greatest fear of his life: failure.

It's been fascinating for me over the years to see how men have responded to the title of this book, *Finding the Hero in Your Husband*. I've had random men at book signings come up to me and desperately ask, "How do I get my wife to read this book?" The title alone gives them hope.

Your husband doesn't just want to be a hero. His emotional and relationship security depends upon becoming a hero. In her classic book *For Women Only*, Shaunti Feldhahn reveals that three out of four men would rather be unloved than disrespected.[i] She also found that more than 80 percent of men said that they were likely to feel disrespected when in conflict with their wives.[ii] Respect is a key to intimacy for men, so it's worth our effort to understand why.

Think of the activities and narratives boys and men are drawn to. From Marvel movies to *The Gladiator*, men love stories of heroes overcoming their vulnerabilities to save the day. And there is always a woman in the story because she compels him to risk. Whether she's in the stands of the Super Bowl or fighting alongside him in the battle against crime, he wants to make her proud.

By becoming a husband, each man enters the ring hoping to be a hero, but secretly he fears he is really a failure.

Do you remember what I wrote about that "puzzle box" in Chapter 1? Your marriage is designed to tell the story of the greatest hero who gave His life to save His Bride. That story is written in the heart of every man. This is the central drama of a man's life.

Just as men dream of being the hero, they also fear becoming the *zero* who lets the whole world down. Your husband was created by God to move into the chaos of the world and make a mark on it for God's glory. To *move* means to risk. By becoming a husband, each man enters the ring hoping to be a hero, but secretly he fears he is really a failure. What about the quarterback who threw an interception or the slugger who struck out to end the big game?

To play the game means taking that risk. Although some men have been raised to project a facade of strength, every man has insecurities around his worth and competence. He may constantly feel the tension to prove that he is good enough.

I know men who are respected and very successful in their work but they still ask questions like, "Am I enough? What if I fail? What if people figure out that I really don't know what I'm doing?" Men can be either driven by this fear of failure or become passive and paralyzed by it. Video games are so attractive because they invite men on the journey to become "heroes" without the risk of failure and humiliation.

And here's where your power comes in.

Although your husband brings to marriage talents and short-comings, his sense of competence is greatly impacted by what he needs from you: your vote of confidence. It's as if every day he wakes up with a silent question for you, his wife: *Do you believe in me?* What makes you even more powerful is that you definitely have the evidence that the answer should be a resounding *NO*. You know your husband's weaknesses and limitations. You've seen him fall short. And so, you have the most informed vote on whether or not he is truly capable of being a hero.

As you grow in intimacy, your husband may share with you aspects of his vulnerability in this area of his heart. Some men, because of childhood experiences and negative messages growing up, bring to marriage the belief that "nothing I ever do will be enough." Your words of encouragement seem to bounce right off him because he has believed in his inadequacy his whole life. But don't give up! Your words, as Proverbs says, have the power to speak life or death.

I've had to learn that even my subtle choice of words or even my tone can make the difference between Mike feeling respected or walked over. I remember one evening early in our marriage coming home with groceries. "I'll make the salad and you grill the burgers," I said casually. My new husband instantly looked offended. "What did you just say? Did you just tell me what to do?"

If I had said the same sentence this way: "I'll make the salad. Would you mind grilling the burgers?" he would have gladly agreed, but something about what I said triggered him. As we talked this out, I learned that Mike loves it when I ask for help but does not like to be told what to do. Even if it wasn't my intention to be bossy, he took it that way. I remember the temptation to argue with him about why he was being so sensitive. That would have gotten us nowhere. Communication is not just what I mean but also how it is being received. Whether or not I'm aware of it, my words (and nonverbals) send a message to my husband of belief or doubt. I have a choice every day to react to the same husband, with the same strengths or weaknesses, with the power to chip away at him or build him up. Now that's power!

Your husband may have different "triggers" that make him feel either disrespected or encouraged. Building intimacy begins with understanding how that sensitivity gives you power. Your wise words can speak assurance into his core fears and life into his soul. No matter how successful or confident a man may seem, he still desperately needs the admiration and approval of his wife.

Oh, it's so tempting to withhold approval and become critical when your husband seems to rightfully deserve it! You might even believe that your critical words and reminders of how he disappoints you will motivate your husband to become a better man. I promise you, the opposite is true. Your husband is drawn to become the man that you reflect to him in the mirror of your feminine soul. No man has ever changed for the better because his wife saw him as a failure, but many have matured to become the hero his wife believed him to be.

Respect is not a feeling but the choice to use your power in a way that builds and believes, even in the face of disappointment.

No man has ever changed for the better because his wife saw him as a failure, but many have matured to become the hero his wife believed him to be.

Need #2: He Needs Your Help

With all the talk about romance and sex, most of us are drawn to marriage because we want a teammate who complements our strengths and steps into our weaknesses.

In the Garden of Eden, God saw that Adam, by himself, was not "complete." After creating Adam, God said, "It is not good for the man to be alone; I will make him a helper suitable for him" (Gen. 2:18 NIV). Eve didn't just keep Adam company as he strolled around the garden. She helped him accomplish the work that God had given him. Together, they were told to "Be fruitful, to multiply and subdue the earth." This work could only be accomplished as a team.

The Hebrew word for helper, *ezer*, doesn't communicate this "helper" as a second-rate assistant. This word *ezer* shows up in the Old Testament twenty-one times. We know that it is used to describe Eve, but it's also used sixteen times to reference God as a helper. This word is always used to refer to a vital and even powerful kind of help. God created women to be a unique aspect of help to humanity, specifically to her own husband.

Let's take a step back for a moment. There is heated discussion in our society about whether gender is a social construct or an innate quality. That argument is not within the scope of this book. I'm going to ask you to accept the premise that God created men and women. Both are made in His image with dignity and strength. They have individual personalities, interests, strengths, and weaknesses that transcend gender. Not every woman likes to cook, and not every man wants to work on cars.

I'm married to a very relational man, and I'm not your stereotypical woman. At times, we've had to take with a grain of salt marriage advice that assumes the woman is the talker, the one who cries, and the spouse who makes decisions emotionally. I'm a thinker more than a feeler. I cry about once a year. And Mike can outtalk me any day of the week. But we are still very much male and female. I am an *ezer* to Mike both in my unique personality traits and in my femininity. Beyond gender stereotypes, God created male and female with essence and nuance that are true to their gender.

The need for a "completer" in marriage naturally gives a wife influence. Without his wife's help and perspective, a man will be less effective at work, with his children, in his relationships, and in knowing himself. A wife's influence and input can be extremely powerful. She teaches him about aspects of life and relationships that would otherwise be lost to him.

If a man's core fear is failure and, alone, he lacks the ability to succeed, then his wife is not only the one who believes in him but also strives alongside him.

Another key aspect of completing is accountability. Ecclesiastes 4:9–10 says: "Two are better than one because they have a good return for their labor. For if either of them falls, the one will lift up his companion. But woe to the one who falls when there is not another to lift him up." As the one who knows your husband's heart, you can uniquely discern his areas of vulnerability and confront him when necessary. (Later in the book, we will look at the difference between this healthy accountability and nagging.)

Remember that a married man and woman are also a brother and sister in Christ. That means a healthy marriage is "iron sharpening iron." We carry each other's burdens (Gal. 6:2) and speak the truth in love when necessary (Eph. 4:15). I can think of many times in our marriage when both Mike and I have needed each other to lift each other up. Whether it is a spiritual struggle, a moral temptation, or just a difficult time, having the other person there has been crucial. Sometimes it was a word of encouragement, a timely warning, or even a kick in the pants. Marriages become dysfunctional and potentially abusive when a woman doesn't use her strength as a guardrail for her husband.

A Tension of Two Needs

Over the years, I've become more aware of how my husband relies on my strengths. I help him understand and communicate with our sons. I'm a sounding board for problems at work. I take care of things that aren't on his radar (and he does the same for me).

This was not always the case. Early in our marriage, my attempts to be an *ezer* were sometimes perceived as a threat.

I grew up in a Christian home, and Mike came to know the Lord in his early twenties. When we got married, I knew the Bible well and had to learn the nuance of what a Christian marriage *is supposed* to look like. Add onto that I had a master's degree in psychology and was completing my doctorate. From my perspective, I had a lot that could *help* my husband with life. But my helping was more like telling Mike why I knew better than he did.

My strengths, particularly the ones Mike needed to become that hero, gave me power. Early on, I used that power to *compete* rather than to *complete*. We got to the point where he was not open to my perspective and well-thought-out advice. There is a tension between a man's need for respect and his need for help. If he relies on your advice, is that a sign of weakness? And if you are constantly offering your "help," won't your husband see that as criticism?

> My strengths, particularly the ones Mike needed to become that hero, gave me power. Early on, I used that power to *compete* rather than to *complete*.

This is a dilemma all women face in marriage. How do you help your husband and respect him at the same time? It's like two wings of an airplane. If one is out of balance with the other, you may be headed for disaster. A wife who only respects and never helps will enable her husband's weaknesses. A wife who never respects and always helps will shut down his strength.

It has helped me to think about these two aspects of my power as a bridge. By encouraging and respecting my husband, I'm laying down planks of wood that help him to trust me. When I help him by sharing my perspective or confronting, I'm putting weight on the bridge. I can only walk as far as I've built.

If your husband doesn't trust that you believe in him, he will be defensive when you offer help. Even your most sincere words will be received as criticism. If you've spent years *helping* your husband, you might need to take some time to build a bridge of trust. Your husband won't be able to receive even your best advice and help if he doesn't first trust your heart for him.

Some women react to this advice by asking, "Why are guys so sensitive? Why do I have to be so careful with my words?" Ironically, these are the same questions men ask when they carelessly trample on their wife's emotional need. God has created us, both male and female, to be vulnerable in intimacy. The triggers of rejection and pain are different, but love means that we go the extra mile to protect rather than to harm each other in marriage.

The triggers of rejection and pain are different, but love means that we go the extra mile to protect rather than to harm each other in marriage.

Need #3: He Needs You to Join Him Sexually

"Anybody who believes that the way to a man's heart is through his stomach flunked geography."[iii] Yes, there is a more powerful love language than your husband's favorite home-cooked meal.

Sexuality is a massive force in a man's life. For many women, this is not a surprising statement. Maybe your husband constantly reminds you that sex is important to him. Other women are puzzled by this power of masculine sexuality. Despite the stereotypes, not all men want sex all the time. There will be seasons in most marriages in which the wife wants sex more often than her husband.

Even if a man has a low sex drive, sexuality is a mysteriously key aspect of what it means to be masculine. Just think of the word *impotent*. It's how we describe a man who can't achieve an erection, but it literally means "without power."

For many men, particularly in their twenties and thirties, physical sexual desire is a driving force. Their bodies are raging with testosterone, and sexual temptation is everywhere. Paul gave the advice that if you "burn" with sexual desire, you should get married.[iv] Even for non-Christian men, having a regular sexual partner is a compelling reason to get married. It's also one of the main reasons men become dissatisfied in marriage.[v] Put simply, for many men sex is the primary way they connect with their wives. Yes, it's physical. But it's also a lot more than that.

A woman's sexual response is notoriously complicated. Many women (and their husbands) view her sexual responsiveness as a great conundrum. Even a woman's anatomy speaks of a mystery to be unveiled and pursued. While a man's physical sex organ is more straightforward (my friend Dr. Jennifer Degler describes it as a glorified water pistol), his sexuality has its own hidden complexity. Because we think of male sexuality as simplistic, we rarely plumb the depth of its power in a man's life.

When women have a simplistic understanding of men and sex, we try to address a physical need without realizing that the power of sex in marriage is far more complicated. As a young wife, I consistently heard that it was my job to make sure that my husband was sexually satisfied so that he wouldn't be tempted by porn or other women. This "gift" became a great burden. For many years of my marriage, I approached sex with fear and guilt rather than understanding the bigger picture of why sex is so important to my marriage.

I recently met with a couple who were frustrated by the lack of sex in their marriage. I asked them "What do you think is the purpose of sex?" The husband said, "It's to have fun and connect with each other." The wife said, "It's how I know that I'm needed." The way this couple viewed sex was all about meeting the husband's need. When they had sex, she often felt used by him and when they didn't have sex, she was afraid he was "getting it somewhere else." The husband felt a constant sense of disappointment that his wife couldn't enjoy sex.

Your husband doesn't *need sex* as much as he needs you to share the journey of sexuality with him. Yes, your female body gives you a certain power that God intended to capture your husband's attention. But the greater power of sexuality is the invitation to be truly known and embraced.

The central drama with men and sex is not just about being sexually satisfied. Your husband's sexuality is the innate prompting for him to pursue intimacy. When male teenagers sexually awaken, their bodies begin screaming, *"You were not made to do life alone!"* Healthy male sexuality is supposed to propel a man to pursue a woman for the purpose of intimacy. Unhealthy male sexuality splits off the experience of sex from this pursuit of intimacy and oneness. It becomes only about the physical release and personal pleasure. A good man not only wants to become one flesh with his wife in body but also wants to be united with her in life. He isn't satisfied with his own sexual pleasure. He also wants to be a "hero lover," able to bring great pleasure to his wife.

In research, Shaunti Feldhahn reported "97 percent of men said 'getting enough sex' wasn't, by itself, enough—they wanted to feel wanted." Her survey showed that "even if they were getting all the sex they wanted, three out of four men would still feel empty if the wife wasn't both engaged and satisfied."[vi]

The average sexual relationship is fraught with emotional land mines. Insecurity. Shame. Fear of rejection. Feeling used. Unspoken temptations. Because of this, we naturally hide from each other. Instead of being "naked and unashamed," we are "guarded and afraid of exposure." We learn to share our bodies but keep our thoughts, fears, and desires a secret.

> Healthy male sexuality is supposed to propel a man to pursue a woman for the purpose of intimacy. Unhealthy male sexuality splits off the experience of sex from this pursuit of intimacy and oneness.

Yes, your husband may say that sex is a significant need for him, but the greater longing is to be known in his sexuality. Even a man who doesn't have a high sex drive may be ashamed of admitting *this* to his wife. Maybe she will think there is something broken in his masculinity if he doesn't want sex all the time. The tendency for men to hide is reinforced by the fact that women are sometimes repelled by male sexuality.

Do you really want to know what your husband struggles with sexually? Have you ever felt disgusted by how men think about sex? Do you believe there is more to your husband's sexuality than his penis and hormones?

> **The power of sex is not primarily in the act, but in the journey of becoming one, creating the safety to share and not be rejected.**

The power of sex is not primarily in the act, but in the journey of becoming one, creating the safety to share and not be rejected. A man's sexuality is yet another venue that determines whether or not he is a hero, and many men feel like a failure in the bedroom. A failure for wanting sex too often or not enough, for climaxing too soon or not soon enough. A failure for not being able to figure out how to please his wife or wounding her with his wrong choices.

Jennifer and Jeremy are an example of how this often plays out in marriage. Together they have three rambunctious children and juggle the many responsibilities of their work and family. They have a good marriage, and Jennifer works hard to make sex a priority in their relationship. She often finds Jeremy to be less than interested in her flirtations. This goes against everything she expected in marriage. When they were dating, they couldn't keep their hands off each other. She's read marriage books that make it sound like every man is desperate for sex with his wife. What's wrong with her?

About every six months, Jennifer stumbles on a browser history or actually catches her husband looking at porn. He downplays it, "I've just been under a lot of stress. It was just a pop-up ad. Honestly, it's not like I've ever paid for porn! It's just a normal struggle guys have."

These exchanges always make her doubt, "Why am I not enough for him? Why would he rather look at porn than be with me?"

Porn offers to make a man feel sexually alive for a moment without the risk of rejection. It's not that she isn't enough, but that *he fears that he is not enough.* Every time Jennifer discovers yet another example of his problem, shame convinces Jeremy to hide even more. He tries even harder to project the man she wants him to be without being honest about the man that he is.

Help for Jennifer and Jeremy is not just about putting a filter on the computer (although this would be a good idea). They will never move past this cycle until Jeremy is willing to risk being known and until Jennifer is courageous enough to know him. You cannot understand your husband sexually until you see it within the lens of who he is emotionally and spiritually. Even the Christian husband who has sex with his wife likely has little idea of how to share more than his body with her or how to take more than her body for his pleasure.

> Using your power in sex well means taking *sexual intimacy* seriously. This doesn't mean you have to have sex all the time. It means respecting the power that sex represents in your relationship.

Yes, the power of sex is physical. But the greater power is the invitation to know your husband and to walk with him on the journey.

Sex is so powerful that it will either divide or unite you in marriage. Using your power in sex well means taking *sexual intimacy* seriously. This doesn't mean you have to have sex all the time. It means respecting the power that sex represents in your relationship. You and your husband must learn to communicate about your needs, desires, and disappointments and take active steps to build this area of your marriage. In Chapter 9, we will look at some practical ways to do this.

Your Power, Your Choice

Whether you are aware of it or not, you have power in your husband's life. Notice that I didn't say you have *control* in your husband's life. You are not responsible for his choices and you cannot change him. But don't let that underestimate the influence God has given you. Your presence has a major impact on your husband's practical, moral, and spiritual decisions every single day. God has given you this power as a wife for the purpose of *building* your house. Your call is to use your strength, beauty, intelligence, and intuition to *empower* your husband.

You might feel very powerless in your marriage. Maybe you married a man who is afraid of being challenged or questioned by you and you've learned to keep the peace by staying quiet. Your feelings of powerlessness may be very real, but that doesn't mean that you don't have power. In fact, your husband may be dominating and controlling because he's actually afraid of your power! Every wife (including you) is making a difference in her husband's life, even through her refusal to use her influence. This means that every wife (including you) must choose whether she will use her influence to build her house or tear it down.

If we are honest, we will admit that we more often end up using our power to stay safe, to express disappointment, and to gain control. Everything in our world that God created has the potential to be distorted. Music can glorify God or profane Him. Money can feed the hungry or destroy the character of a nation. The law can protect the innocent or restrict freedom. A woman's power is no exception to this rule. What God intended for good has been used by some to destroy His design for marriage and oneness. We never use our power well unless we intentionally pursue doing so. Each of us is naturally a lot more like that foolish wife who tears down her home rather than the wise one who builds it up.

Your Power Source

As you learn about how to use your power as a wife, you may wonder who will empower *you*. Where do you run with your frustrations and longings if you are focused on investing in your marriage?

Remember what you read about being an *ezer*? You also have an *ezer*. You are not in this alone. The Greek word in the Bible that is used for power is *dunamis*, which is where we get the word *dynamite*. Here are some definitions of what that word means: force (literally or figuratively); specially, miraculous power (usually by implication, a miracle itself); ability, abundance, meaning, might, (worker of) miracle(-s), power, strength, mighty (wonderful) work.[vii]

This is the strength and power that God gives to people who are surrendered to His work. When I grow weary in my marriage or ministry, I need to remember that I am empowered by the Spirit of God Himself. I am saved by this power (Rom. 1:16), kept by it (I Peter 1:5), strengthened in it (Eph. 3:16), equipped through it (2 Peter 1:3), and I have hope because of it (Rom. 15:13).

Yes, you have power as a wife. But you have a far greater power through surrendering to the work of Jesus Christ in your life and your marriage. In the chapters that follow, I will challenge you to consider how you use your power as a wife. Please remember that God will not ask you to do something without also equipping you to do it.

Endnotes

i Shaunti Feldhahn, *For Women Only* (OR: Multnomah Publishers, 2004). p. 23.

ii Feldhahn, p. 25.

iii This quote is attributed to Robert Byrnes. I had trouble finding an original source.

iv I Corinthians 7:9.

v https://www.ncbi.nlm.nih.gov/pmc/articles/PMC4105603/.

vi Feldhahn, pp. 93–94.

vii https://www.bibletools.org/index.cfm/fuseaction/Lexicon.show/ID/G1411 /dunamis.htm.

♥

Chapter 3

nobody told me that marriage could be so lonely

In today's modern world, we no longer get married because of cultural norms or financial stability. The driving force behind marriage is to be united with another person. You want a husband to share the journey of life. Marriage means no more lonely weekend nights all by yourself. You get to sleep with your best friend, have meaningful conversations, and problem solve together.

At least that's what we hope marriage will be. But what if it's not?

Nothing feels lonelier than when there is emotional distance or conflict between my husband and me. The tension of living in the same physical space with someone who feels like a stranger and putting on fake smiles in public is excruciating. Over time, some couples just accept this tension and learn to live in the stalemate of marriage without meaningful connection.

Marriage is based on the covenant promise you and your husband made to each other. That covenant is a promise of faithfulness meant to move you toward intimacy. Remember that marriage is a reflection of God's covenant love. Just as a husband and wife were not intended to live insulated from each other, God designed each of us for an intimate relationship with Him. A negotiated peace treaty of married "roommates" is better than open tension but falls short of God's design for your marriage.

In general, we as women tend to be more vocal about our desire for deeper intimacy within marriage. I've heard hundreds of women over the years say things like "I just don't know how to connect to his heart" or "He says he loves me but he never really listens to me." If I ask a husband and wife to individually rate their marriage on a scale from one to ten, the woman is almost always the one who rates it lower. Why? Because she generally longs for more and is aware of the gaps in their connection. If your marriage is a car, then you are likely to be the first to notice the "check engine light." If you bring it up, your husband might even respond with "Everything sounds good to me. Let's just keep driving it until something is obviously broken."

This can make you think that you are the only one in the marriage who wants or needs intimacy.

Husbands Need Intimacy, Too

How would your husband respond if you began a conversation with "Let's talk about us"? Would he eagerly jump in or stare back at you like a deer caught in the headlights?

Gender differences might be all but eliminated in most social or work settings. However, the vulnerability and intensity of marriage strips away casual scripts and exposes the raw needs of men and women.

In the last chapter, we looked at a man's foundational needs in marriage, including his longing to be your hero. Let's relate this to working on intimacy in your marriage. When you approach your husband with the question, "Can we talk about us?" his natural internal response will likely be *"Oh, no. Now I get to hear about what I'm doing wrong."*

One foundational gender difference is that men tend to be more focused on mastering their world and achieving goals while women are more oriented toward inviting and nurturing relationships. This doesn't mean that women can't find great satisfaction in work or that men can't be

> For a woman, the success of marriage means feeling close and connected. For a man, it usually is linked to being a good husband (a hero).

fulfilled through their relationships, but that they approach these aspects of life differently. For a woman, the success of marriage means feeling close and connected. For a man, it usually is linked to being a good husband (a hero). He is wired to want to make you happy even though he might not know how to accomplish this goal.

This difference between husbands and wives is glaringly obvious when the couple seeks help in counseling. Tearfully, the wife makes the call, desperate for more in her marriage. "Why can't he understand how much his apathy hurts me? All I ask for is a little sensitivity!" When he finally joins her for counseling, the man often says something like "No matter what I do, I can't make her happy." He states his case that the happy-go-lucky girl he fell in love with is now more like his shift manager. "Nothing I do is ever good enough."

Even a man's most intimate relationships will be viewed within the framework of competence. Saying "I want to work on our marriage" is not typically heard as an invitation to deeper intimacy, but as a criticism for how he is failing you. He's not going to be fulfilled in marriage unless he is your hero. Early in your relationship this was probably easy. When you fell in love, his attention was on you and your expectations for him were far lower. Now it's more complicated. To put it simply, you expect more from him. And he's no longer trying to "win" you.

I remember talking to one young husband who looked into his wife's eyes and said, "I am going to tell you right now that I love you. Remember it. Until you hear differently, just assume that I love you." As you might have guessed, this wasn't received as a romantic gesture by his wife. She felt like he was "checking the box" of being a good husband, not pursuing her heart. It may feel defeating or annoying when a wife is asking for a deeper connection with her husband, but this is also a gift from God. Because a woman is typically more wired to pursue intimacy, she provides an important reminder for *both of them* to work on their marriage and not settle for a superficial friendship. If a wife gives up on trying to establish intimacy, in many cases the marriage will disintegrate into open conflict or a dynamic of polite coworkers.

A woman's greater focus on relationships and connection does not mean that only females need intimacy. Although they may not make it a stated goal, men need intimacy, too. While men don't usually like to *talk* about intimacy, that doesn't mean that they don't crave it. As crazy as it sounds, a man might run from intimacy and seek it at the same time. This is in large part because he doesn't know how to achieve it, and a man will naturally avoid something he's not already good at.

By the Way, What Is Intimacy?

Intimacy. It is a word we throw around all the time. As much as we use it, do we really know what it means to experience intimacy? A lot of people immediately think of sex when talking about intimacy, but sex and intimacy are not the same thing. You can have sex with someone without any intimacy, and you can be intimate with someone in a way that is not at all sexual.

The word *intimate* comes from a Latin word that means "innermost."[i] It's the idea of knowing someone in their innermost self and embracing them completely. Building intimacy involves two people who are willing to disclose at the risk of becoming vulnerable. There are three important components to intimacy: willingness, disclosure, and vulnerability.

First of all, intimacy the willingness to move toward each other in a meaningful way.

Intimacy will never happen if only one person wants it. There is a difference between a husband who doesn't know how to be intimate and one who has no interest in it.

I recently talked with a woman who described her seven-year marriage as perpetual grief and loneliness. Her husband from day one flirted with other women, lied about money, and dismissed her feelings whenever she brought up these concerns. Recovering from yet another affair, she desperately wants to fix their marriage. Her husband is willing to go through counseling. He is sorry for getting caught and wants the security of his marriage, but still, he blames his wife for being controlling and pushing him into the arms of another woman. I grieved with this woman, helping her understand that her husband was likely never interested in intimacy. Unless the Lord breaks this man, there is little chance of building any sense of true connection in their relationship.

Both must be willing and wanting to seek it, even if they don't know how to get there. Most marriage counselors will tell you they enjoy working with any two people who genuinely desire intimacy with each other. There is more hope for a couple who both have big problems but open hearts than for a couple with minor problems and someone with a hard heart.

Intimacy requires disclosure. Think about how the physical process of sexual intimacy mirrors the process of emotional intimacy. In sexual intimacy, you completely share your body with your husband. This usually means you get naked physically. Obviously, taking off your clothes is only appropriate within the context of trust and familiarity. While sex is the extreme end of getting naked, you are comfortable "disrobing" at various levels depending on how safe and familiar you feel with people. You don't think twice about taking off a coat or jacket in public. In front of friends, you probably kick off your shoes. When you're with your best friends or family, you might walk around in a robe or PJs. But only in the context of true intimacy do you expose your entire body to your partner to study and enjoy.

To become emotionally intimate, you have to be willing to remove your "emotional clothing." When you first met your husband, you probably "put your toe in the waters" of intimacy by telling pieces of your story and showing him some of your heart. Over time, you learned to trust each other with more of yourselves, becoming less guarded. Moving toward deeper intimacy within your marriage requires that you learn to disclose even more.

Intimacy requires vulnerability. When a man shares his innermost hopes and fears, he becomes defenseless. When a woman communicates how she feels and what she longs for, she is open to rejection and hurt. There is no way to avoid the risk that inherently comes with intimacy. To achieve ultimate intimacy means to risk ultimate vulnerability. Although men and women desperately want and need intimacy, they will hit barriers when the risk of being exposed outweighs the desire to be known.

> Although men and women desperately want and need intimacy, they will hit barriers when the risk of being exposed outweighs the desire to be known.

It Is Better to Be Safe Than Close

The concept of vulnerability helps to explain why men may be more likely than women to avoid intimacy, even within the context of marriage. From the time we were little girls, we were encouraged to share our feelings. Females have BFFs and generally learn to talk through conflicts at a young age. Male friendships, even in childhood, are usually more defined by common interests than connection with one another. In general, men want to *do life* together while women want to *process life* together.

This makes women generally better at the skills required for intimacy. They are usually far more comfortable expressing and discussing their feelings, which is necessary to becoming emotionally intimate. In other words, when it comes to relationships, women have home court advantage. People take risks when they feel comfortable about their ability to cover the risk. If a man is not confident in the arena of close relationships, risking vulnerability makes no sense to him. He decides, "It is better to be safe than to be known."

You can probably define the problems in your marriage in many different ways, but they ultimately boil down to you and/ or your husband not feeling safe enough to keep moving toward each other. The process of building intimacy means making the daily choice to push into unity rather than to stay guarded. If the environment of a marriage isn't safe for both people, then it can't be intimate.

> The process of building intimacy means making the daily choice to push into unity rather than to stay guarded.

Intimacy requires that both of you meet each other at the deepest point of your need. Exposing your needs means that you can be hurt. Let's face it. Relationships, especially close ones, can be very scary. All of us have experienced the pain of rejection or abandonment sometime throughout our lives and likely even within our marriages. Those painful lessons stick with us and motivate us to avoid feeling vulnerable.

Ultimately, for emotional intimacy to grow, each partner must be willing to meet the other's needs and protect the other's greatest vulnerability. This produces an environment of trust, allowing both of you to feel safe to share more. But when vulnerability is met with rejection and pain, you will naturally move away from sharing and toward self-protection.

And this is where we come back to the importance of understanding relational power.

What You Need to Be Intimate

In the last chapter, we looked at three specific needs that your husband has brought into your marriage: He needs your respect, your help, and your companionship on the journey of sexuality. Each of these needs presents the opportunity for intimacy or for hurt. You learned how his needs give you power in your relationship.

The same is true of your needs. They naturally make you vulnerable, giving your husband power to build or to destroy intimacy.

If he meets your needs, you feel safe. If he doesn't, you put up walls.

I'm sure you've heard the jokes about how complicated and *needy* women are. Ultimately, our core needs in marriage boil down to two words: value and protection. Picture a delicate, beautifully crafted vase. With its unique grooves in the crystal, there is only one like it in the world. To fulfill the purpose for which this vase was designed, its value must be appreciated and its delicacy protected. This precious, fragile vase is very similar to a married woman.

I love how Peter mentions these two aspects of wives as he instructs married men: "Husbands, treat your wives with consideration as a delicate vessel, and with honor as fellow heirs of the gracious gift of life, so that your prayers will not be hindered."[ii]

These two core needs, value and protection, are critical to intimacy in your marriage. They give your husband the power to either meet your needs or to cause you to feel constantly on guard.

The first thing a wife needs to emotionally thrive in marriage is to be valued or cherished by her husband. When I try to describe this to men, I tell them to imagine being the only man in a room filled with thousands of women. Among the thousands is your wife. She wants to know that you chose and will continue to choose her. Even if she's not the most beautiful, the smartest, or the best in bed, you want to be exclusively with her. Her greatest fear isn't failure but rejection. This rejection can take many forms (work, looking at porn, ignoring her) but always communicates the same thought: *"You are no longer my first choice."* When a woman takes the risk of intimacy and allows her husband to know what is behind the masks she wears, she is open to either deep love or the ultimate rejection.

While a man thinks he only has to pursue his wife to "win" her once, a woman wants to be continually pursued. This is symbolic of his love and interest in her. The need to feel greatly valued explains why a woman may be wounded by simple things her husband might choose, particularly if their relationship isn't in a good place. When he consistently chooses to spend his days off with friends, his wife might interpret this as *"He values his friends more than he values me."* If a man spends sixty-five hours a week at work, his wife may think that his work is more important than their relationship. Spending $8,000 on a new motorcycle means he would rather spend his money on boy toys than on the love of his life.

The second emotional need for a woman in marriage is to feel secure. You can make the argument that in many ways, women are as strong as men. Both science and history have proven the incredible physical and emotional resources of women. However, being feminine in many respects means being vulnerable. Just think of the physical picture of sexual intimacy. A woman opens herself up to be penetrated. To be sexually intimate, she must be willing to become vulnerable. A good man will always honor her willingness to open herself, but this exposure means the risk of harm.

While a woman can take care of herself, she doesn't want to have to. Women are overwhelmingly more at risk for domestic violence, sexual assault, and other violent crimes, including within intimate relationships.[iii] Unfortunately, a man's booming voice, powerful muscles, and stature can be used to intimidate rather than to protect. In order for intimacy to occur in marriage, a woman must be absolutely certain that her husband's strength will be used to protect rather than to harm.

A woman's need for protection goes beyond the physical aspect. While a woman can take care of herself, she doesn't want to have to. One of the greatest complaints I've heard from wives is that their husbands won't step up: he won't lead spiritually; he won't provide financially; he leaves her to discipline the kids. Yes, she can do all these things, but at the expense of flourishing in marriage. When a woman has to be "tough" for the sake of her survival, she sacrifices her unique ability to connect emotionally with those she loves.

A man who values his wife but refuses to step up and be the hero has neglected one of her core needs.

What about sex? You may notice that I specifically mentioned sharing the sexual journey as a core need for men but not for women. There are many marriages in which the wife expresses more sexual desire than her husband. So, what gives?

For many women (not all), sex is not viewed as a separate need but more as an expression of feeling loved and valued. The same argument can be made for male sexuality... Perhaps it's not so much a separate need but an extension of feeling respected and completed. However, men are much more likely than women to mention sex as an important need in marriage. The average man has ten to twenty times the testosterone level than the average woman,[iv] making physical sexual desire usually more of a felt need within romantic relationships.

The Cycle of Intimacy

Let's put this puzzle of marriage together. Men come in with needs that give the wife power; women come in with needs that give the husband power. Intimacy happens when they both use their power to meet the other's needs. Women need to be valued and protected while men need to be respected and completed. In marriage, a wife is vulnerable to being seen as unlovable and a husband is vulnerable to being seen as incompetent. The primary message to husbands in the Bible can be summed up by "love your wife." The central message to wives is "respect your husband." Do you see how God's unique instructions to husband and wife overlap with their deepest needs? God's design for marriage intrinsically supports a cycle of growing intimacy. It helps the husband and wife use their power well.

When both the husband and wife use their relational power to meet each other's needs, intimacy will steadily deepen. The more he meets her needs, the more likely she is to meet his. It's a perpetual cycle, one I've experienced many seasons in my marriage. Let me give you an example of how this works.

My husband, Mike, knows me intimately. Because I am a reserved person, he knows that it takes time for me to share my thoughts with him. When we go on walks together, he often asks me questions to get me to talk. He is patient when I give him short answers instead of diving into what I'm really thinking. This shows me that he loves me enough to pursue my heart.

Mike also protects me. He knows that I'm super intense and often overcommit to the point of exhaustion. (We have had many "discussions" about this in our marriage!) In the early days, his fun-loving personality honestly used to annoy me. I wished he would be more serious, too. As a young wife, I fought against his input. Who was he to speak about my schedule? But I've learned that Mike is God's provision for my needs. He protects me from myself by prompting me to stop working and helping me put up boundaries with ministry and travel.

When I think about how my husband values and protects me, I am grateful for him. I'm not quickly annoyed even when we have disagreements because I appreciate him. It's easy to see him as a hero when my focus is on how he loves and takes care of me. When I feel that way about Mike, I naturally want to do whatever I can to help him in his work and relationships. His love toward me motivates me to be a wife who encourages and fulfills him.

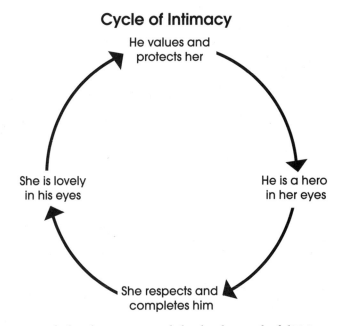

Cycle of Intimacy

He values and protects her

He is a hero in her eyes

She respects and completes him

She is lovely in his eyes

Doesn't this dynamic sound absolutely wonderful? Men yearn for this intimacy as much as women do. The challenge is that few marriages can sustain this cycle of intimacy. Unfortunately, life gets in the way. No matter how sensitive and well-meaning you may be, every husband and wife will fail within the intensity of intimacy. Try as you might, it is impossible to always meet each other's needs and never tread on each other's vulnerability. Husbands and wives are, after all, only human. In the daily interchange of marriage there are hundreds of opportunities to either build trust or tear it down. In good marriages, most of those opportunities result in responding to needs and protecting each other from harm. But every couple faces the inevitable betrayal of trust, whether intentional or not. It happens every day, in big ways and small. And this is where the disappointment settles in.

The Cycle of Self-Protection

Have you ever made your husband's favorite dinner only to have him say, "Thanks, but I already ate"? Or did you ever start telling your husband about your day and he wandered away in the middle of your sentence? And what about your part in this dance...like rolling your eyes at your husband's attempt at parenting, or dismissing his ideas about how to solve a problem? These are little examples of how you can very quickly get bumped off the cycle of intimacy.

These small hurts and breaches of trust are what ultimately lead many to marital devastation. Scott Stanley's research in *Fighting for Your Marriage* concluded that the greatest predictor of marital success and failure is how a couple deals with the little conflicts that they encounter every day.[v] In the long run, what may matter most is how the couple recovers intimacy when they have children throwing up in the middle of the night, when he says something that hurts her feelings, or when she says something critical about him in front of his friends. These little things bump a couple off the cycle of intimacy and onto a cycle of defensiveness. Guarding against additional hurt, each person seeks self-protection. Both become less concerned with meeting the other's needs. Instead, they succumb to the temptation to exploit the other's vulnerability because *the exploiter becomes more powerful and safer than the victim.* The big breaches of trust (like infidelity, secret spending, and slinging cruel words) sometimes result from years of smaller, unaddressed conflicts that end up building massive walls between a husband and wife.

The cycle of self-protection is the exact opposite of God's design for intimacy in marriage. Mike and I have spent our share of time on this cycle of self-protection. Let me tell you a story about how easily this can happen.

I'm one of those people who likes to get everywhere early. Arriving on time feels late to me. As chance would have it, I married a man who considers it a challenge to be always running late and make it just on time. Most Sundays, this drama plays out on the way to church.

I remember one particular Sunday waiting in the kitchen for my husband and three boys to leave for church. Of course, we were running late, but my husband assured me, "Buckle up. I'll get you there on time!" And so, he proceeded to drive (in my opinion) recklessly and (based on the speed limit) way too fast to church. These were not the "heroics" I was hoping for. As we approached a yellow (turning red) light, I could feel my husband accelerating. I was already on edge, quietly fuming at his driving and the fact that we were late for church. I screamed "STOP!" Mike jammed on the breaks right at the red light and said a not-so-nice curse word. Out my mouth came "Great, Mike. Wonderful example in front of the boys!"

Neither of us woke up that morning with the intention of fighting. But by the time we got to church, we wanted to sit on opposite sides of the sanctuary. What happened? How did we so quickly go from intimacy to hostility?

Let's begin with my reaction to Mike being late to church and then driving like a madman to get us there. I felt devalued (*He knows I hate being late for church. If he really loved me, he would make the effort.)* and not protected, *(He's going to kill us by his NASCAR stunts! And what kind of spiritual leader would swear in front of his wife and kids?)* Even before that, Mike probably felt like I was nagging him to be ready for church on time, *(I'm not one of the kids that she can boss around. I'll be ready when I'm ready. We'll only miss some of the singing. And hey, I'm going to church. Shouldn't that count for something?)* My reaction to the stoplight only poured fuel on the fire. Mike's kind and wonderful wife very quickly became a critical, closed off, bossy woman. The last thing he wanted to do was show me love and affection, and the last thing I wanted to do was treat him with respect.

With your own circumstances and personalities, I'm guessing this same thing happens in your marriage. It looks like this:

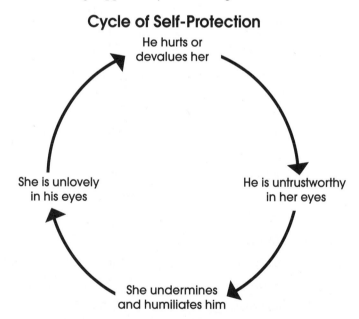

Cycle of Self-Protection

He hurts or devalues her

He is untrustworthy in her eyes

She undermines and humiliates him

She is unlovely in his eyes

Every marriage is on one of these two cycles at any given time. In a healthy marriage, you can learn to quickly repair the breach in trust and get back on the cycle of intimacy. Early in our marriage, that fight on the way to church might have meant a week of chilly interactions. The pain of experience has taught us to recognize how we got off track and how to intentionally use our relational power to get back to pursuing intimacy.

Maybe you've spent years in self-protection mode. Or maybe you are reeling from a huge breach of trust. Your husband forgetting your anniversary is not the same thing as him sleeping with another woman. The latter can't be fixed with flowers and an apology. Massive wounds in marriage, like deception and betrayal, take willing hearts and years of work to rebuild the kind of trust needed for intimacy to flourish. I know many couples who have experienced the earthquake of affairs, sexual addiction, and raging fights. I've seen God bring healing to the most broken marriages, but only once the husband and the wife begin the real work of vulnerability, repentance, forgiveness, and learning to love.

Where Do We Begin?

"Is it too late for us?" a tearful Shelby asked me. "We've been married for twelve years and I realize now that we've been doing this all wrong. We both have used our power to hurt each other."

The brilliant thing about a cycle is that it can be changed at any point. Yes, it would be wonderful if the Holy Spirit zapped your husband. Pray for that to happen, but you can only impact the cycle by addressing how *you* are using *your* power to build or sabotage intimacy. And remember...your power is connected to *his* needs. You don't have any power in your marriage when you focus on your needs not being met.

Your power is connected to *his* needs. You don't have any power in your marriage when you focus on your needs not being met.

I first met Shelby when she and her husband were in a bad spot in their marriage. She was ready to give up. Shelby explained that she had worked hard to increase intimacy in their marriage. She was the one who came to counseling. She tried everything she knew to do to improve their relationship. But here's the problem: She was trying to draw Robby into intimacy the way she would like to be approached. Shelby assumed that her husband needed to feel valued and loved in the way that she yearned to be. She did this by trying to ask about his day, telling him that she wanted to be closer to him, and sharing her hopes and feelings with him. Her attempts to draw Robby closer usually made him even more distant.

Shelby had to learn how to intervene at her point of power in the cycle of intimacy. More than feeling loved, Robby needed to feel competent and respected as her husband. As a guy who was struggling in his career, Robby didn't want to talk about work. Every time Shelby asked him about his job, he felt like she was checking in on him. When she gave him work advice, he felt belittled.

Shelby began to realize that many of her attempts to draw Robby into intimacy were actually threatening to him. By sharing her desire to be closer to him, she was telling Robby that he wasn't cutting it as a husband. Robby's reaction was *"Great. I'm failing at work and now I'm failing at home, too."*

Things started to change as Shelby took small steps to empower Robby. She asked herself the question, "How can I use my power to connect with my husband?" Instead of always talking, she took an interest in a few of Robby's projects and hobbies. (It turns out, Robby is far more talkative when he's doing something than when he's sitting on a couch with Shelby's eyes boring into him.) She learned to ask Robby for his opinion and help with some problems she was facing. Instead of waiting to feel emotionally close, Shelby sent Robby flirty texts and focused on connecting with him sexually, which is a main way he experienced closeness. Within a short period of time, Robby responded by wanting to spend time with his wife.

Shelby used her influence to change the cycle of her marriage. She set aside her needs *temporarily* in order to focus on her husband's feelings of isolation. She took the risk of vulnerability by initiating closeness in ways Robby would appreciate; she addressed her husband's deepest needs.

Every marriage is in either the cycle of intimacy or the cycle of self-protection. Momentum is either drawing husband and wife toward greater trust or repelling them further into their recesses of self-protection. It only takes one person to change that momentum and begin a new cycle. Just as one cutting remark can spoil the feeling of safety and intimacy, so can a small gesture of trust and vulnerability prepare the relationship for growth.

It may be very difficult for you to imagine how your marriage can get off a perpetual cycle of defensiveness and disappointment. Please know that you are not alone! Keep reading as we dig into what it practically looks like to use your power in ways that promote intimacy.

> **Every marriage is in either the cycle of intimacy or the cycle of self-protection. It only takes one person to change that momentum and begin a new cycle.**

Connecting with the Real Hero

I mentioned at the beginning of this chapter that your relationship with God is meant to be an intimate one. Marriage was created to be a picture or echo of the true intimacy God designed you for. Yet most Christians have a hard time thinking about being "intimate" with God. You may see Him as a stern Father or a watchful judge, not an intimate husband. But the Bible says that this great and Holy God sent Jesus in the flesh to become the Husband of the church! Yes, that applies to the big church filled with lots of people, but it also applies to you as an individual.

When you put your trust in God, He adopts you into His family as a beloved daughter. He protects and loves you as a faithful Husband. He guides you like a caring shepherd. These earthly pictures of intimacy point to the depth of deep intimacy God created for you to have with Him.

I hope that you have placed your trust in Jesus Christ as your Savior. But don't stop there! The apostle Paul prayed for the first Christians to grow in their love and knowledge of God. Growing as a Christian is not just about the learning that happens in your head. It's also about learning to know and trust God as a Being, not just as a concept.

If you only pursue intimacy with your husband, someday you will come up empty. You have depths of longing that no husband can ever fully satisfy. And so, my friend, I urge you to pursue both intimacy with your hero and with the Hero, the Lover of your soul.

Endnotes

i   https://www.etymonline.com/word/intimate.

ii I Peter 3:7.

iii https://ncadv.org/STATISTICS.

iv https://www.healthline.com/health/womens-health/do-women-have
    -testosterone#:~:text=In%20men%2C%20testosterone%20is%20mainly,
    of%20testosterone%20as%20men's%20bodies.

v   Scott Stanley, Howard Markman, Susan Blumberg, *Fighting for Your Marriage* (PA: Wiley, 2001).

♥

Chapter 4

god works in
mysterious ways

In my job speaking on topics of sexuality, I've had to address a lot of uncomfortable and controversial issues. But nothing quite as offensive as what we are covering in this chapter... submission. You might even be internally cringing as I use that word throughout this chapter because it's a trigger for a lot of women. I get it. It's actually easier for me to answer questions about masturbation and sex toys than to wade into these emotionally charged waters.

When I stumble across such unpopular teachings in the Bible, I'm honestly tempted to skip right past them and focus on the passages on which we can all agree. Why not just camp out in I Corinthians 13 (the love chapter)? In truth, you can't write a Christian marriage book without tackling the subject of submission. It shows up in most of the biblical passages that address marriage. So, I either need to prove to you why this teaching is out of date so you can dismiss it, or I need to make the case that a loving God, the Creator of marriage, still intends for wives to submit to their husbands.

Like many biblical principles, this one may apply differently in our current day than it did to a first century Jewish believer who was considered the property of her husband. I hope to convince you that not only is submission relevant to you as a wife in the twenty-first century, but that it is also a key to both intimacy in your marriage and intimacy with God.

We need to understand that submission is not just a lofty topic for theologians to debate. It has incredibly practical implications in the real-world exchanges of marriage. When we get this wrong, we will get marriage wrong. How does a wife who wants to honor God react to these situations?

Tina's husband, Jim, has a bad temper. He sometimes yells at the children when he is frustrated with them or while he's wrestling with a household project. The kids are obviously hurt by his anger and insensitivity. Should Tina intervene? How can she do this in the spirit of submission?

Sam has never been happy at work. Over the course of ten years, he has had nine different jobs and moved his family seven times. Should his wife Laura continue to follow him every time he becomes discontent at work? If she does, is she being submissive or foolish? Should she even tell Sam her objections and concerns? Should she give him an ultimatum?

Jamie, Ashley's husband, uses very little discretion when it comes to what his kids watch. He often streams mature content right in front of their young children. Although Ashley is bothered by Jamie's insensitivity, she doesn't know how to put her foot down. She's mentioned it a few times, but he always dismisses her. She has read about the importance of having a "submissive and quiet spirit." What should she do?

You might imagine that submission in each of these scenarios looks like the wife keeping her mouth shut and putting on a happy face while she internally brews about her husband's irresponsible actions. Actually, that is the opposite of submission. Submitting to your husband is less about what you say or don't say to your husband and much more about the spirit of your heart toward him. In fact, the wife who speaks up in these scenarios may have more of a submissive heart than the one who quietly bottles up her resentment as her husband makes very "unheroic" decisions.

> Submitting to your husband is less about what you say or don't say to your husband and much more about the spirit of your heart toward him.

What I'd like you to consider is that *submission is God's guidance to you as a wife for how to use your power.*

What Submission Is Not

I have Christian friends who strongly disagree with the idea of biblical submission for today's marriage. When we talk through this topic, they point to all the ways teaching on submission has devalued women and put them in a position of vulnerability. We all know stories of women who have been minimized and disregarded by men who thought they were following God's Word by silencing women in the church and Christian family.

These friends will readily agree that men and women are different and that God designed us to complement each other. But the application of that teaching has led to unhealthy marriages and even justified emotional, spiritual, physical, and sexual abuse. This is a sound reason for many Christians to reject the whole idea of submission when it has been so destructive and dishonoring to women. So, before we even define what submission really *is*, let's begin with what it *is not*.

Submission Does Not Mean That Women Are Less Capable Than Men

As a young wife, one of the things that confused me about submission was knowing that I was smart. It won't offend my husband to admit that I'm intellectually deeper than he is. There are certainly many ways his common sense and relational skills outweigh mine, but I have always been a natural thinker. I was that strange kid who couldn't wait for school to start, finished tests twenty minutes before the rest of the class, and loved debating with my professors. So, when we got married, was I supposed to "act stupid" for the sake of my husband's ego? And what about all the biblical knowledge I'd accumulated going to Christian school and church my whole life? Should I play dumb rather than upstage my husband? And how about our dreams and goals? Were Mike's more important to God than mine just because he is male and I'm female?

> I don't believe that God wants me to bury any of the gifts He's given me under the banner of submission. In fact, doing so would go directly against biblical teaching that encourages me to invest my "talents" in the kingdom of God.

The traditional models of submission, like on the old sitcoms, have a sweet little Mrs. at home baking cookies while the Mr. has the real work in the real world. No wonder we struggle to make sense of submission in today's culture!

Submission is not some yoke of inferiority that I put on when I step across the threshold of my home. I don't believe that God wants me to bury any of the gifts He's given me under the banner of submission. In fact, doing so would go directly against biblical teaching that encourages me to invest my "talents" in the kingdom of God.[i]

Understood within the cultural context, the Scriptures paint a picture that highly values femininity. The Bible states clearly that both men and women were created in the image of God. Both Adam and Eve together were charged with subduing the earth.[ii] Although men and women are different in many respects, they are the same in their status as a special creation. Both were set apart as distinct from all of God's other creations. Men and women uniquely express aspects of God's character through their ability to choose, their eternal souls, and their creative abilities.

> Submission is not primarily about being male and female within the larger context of culture. It is the recognition that marriage is a special form of revelation.

We also need to recognize that the Bible does not say "women, submit to men." It says, "wives submit to your own husbands." Submission is not primarily about being male and female within the larger context of culture. It is the recognition that marriage is a special form of revelation. (We will get to more of that later.)

Submission Does Not Mean That Women Should Be Silent

One day I was driving in the car listening to a Christian radio station when I heard something that made me want to scream. A lady who was teaching on submission said emphatically that a woman should never give her opinion on anything unless her husband asks for it. In one sense, I can guess why she gave that marriage advice. Men usually do react badly when their wives are constantly telling them what to do and second-guessing their decisions. But I believe there are many situations in which a woman should give her opinion, even if it is unsolicited.

One of the reasons people believe this application of submission is because of Peter's description of a godly wife in I Peter. Let's take a look at it:

> Wives, in the same way submit yourselves to your own husbands so that, if any of them do not believe the word, they may be won over without words by the behavior of their wives, **if** they see the purity and reverence of your lives. Your beauty should not come from outward adornment, such as elaborate hairstyles and the wearing of gold jewelry or fine clothes. Rather, it should be that of your inner self, the unfading beauty of a gentle and quiet spirit, which is of great worth in God's sight. For this is the way the holy women of the past who put their hope in God used to adorn themselves. They submitted themselves to their own husbands, **if** Sarah, who obeyed Abraham and called him her lord. You are her daughters if you do what is right and do not give way to fear. (I Peter 3:1–6 NIV emphasis added)

Notice that Peter begins verse 1 with "Wives, in the same way..." This was originally a letter that didn't have chapters, and so Peter is referring to what he wrote at the end of Chapter 2. The context of this teaching is using the example of Jesus Christ who endured hardship and even insults for the greater good of glorifying God. In Chapter 3, Peter is specifically talking to godly wives about the hardship of being married to an "unheroic husband." Please notice that he is telling these wives how to be *powerful* in winning them over, not how to be weak in letting them do whatever they want. Also notice that he is teaching them about the nature of their spirit. The "gentle and quiet" spirit describes your internal confidence, not whether or not your mouth is moving. Peter uses Sarah, Abraham's wife, as an example.

Sarah was a lot of things, but she certainly wasn't quiet. Although Sarah clearly followed Abraham's leadership, the Bible includes at least two specific times when she gave her unsolicited opinion.[iii]

Sarah, our example of a submissive woman, obviously played an active role in her marriage. When you read about this ancient marriage, she was downright feisty, particularly given the culture they lived in. Sarah respected Abraham and yielded to God's work in his life, but she did not withhold her feelings and opinions. In at least one instance, God encouraged Abraham to listen to her.[iv]

This imperfect wife is held out as a role model because she wasn't driven by fear, but, like her husband, she had to learn to trust the sovereignty of God.

> It's not whether she's using her voice, but how she's using her power that defines a gentle and quiet spirit.

The voice of women is very necessary both within the Christian home and church. It's not whether she's using her voice, but how she's using her power that defines a gentle and quiet spirit.

"I am a loud, opinionated person!" a woman once told me. "It may be easy for you to have a 'submissive and quiet spirit,' but it is impossible for me!" It is easy to think of a submissive woman as one who is always respectful, ladylike, courteous, and soft-spoken. Not so! A woman is not submissive because she is quiet and refined. No matter her personality, *her spirit* will either stubbornly seek her own way or willingly yield when submission is appropriate. Any woman can be submissive. In fact, Scripture is clear that God's design for marriage is for all husbands and wives—not just for the ones who fit a mold.

Submission Does Not Mean Blind Obedience

The words *submission* and *obedience* are often used interchangeably. In fact, less than a century ago, wedding vows often used the word *obey* rather than *submit*. This is a mistake because the Greek words for *obey* and *submit* are different and communicate different messages.

The word translated as *obey* is used to describe the relationship between children and their parents. To obey means to listen and act without questioning the recognized authority. In contrast, submission is a willing act of placing oneself under the authority of another. Christ is our perfect example of submission. He willingly submitted His desire to His Father's authority by coming to Earth, suffering, and dying on the cross.

Parents have authority over their young children because they have wisdom and understanding that their children lack. A three-year-old has no concept of why he needs to eat vegetables. Even if you tell your child that eating healthy will help him to grow stronger, his little mind has a very limited understanding of the importance of nutrition. At this point in his life, his reasoning does not count. He has to trust in the goodness of his parents. Even teenagers lack the experience, discernment, and the mental capacity to make wise long-term decisions. God has put them under authority to protect them from their own foolishness.

A wife, on the other hand, is a different situation. She has the same ability to reason and make moral and responsible decisions as her husband. She can, in fact, think quite well for herself. Submitting to her husband doesn't mean she turns off her brain. Rather than "obeying," she willingly and thoughtfully yields.

The law reflects this important distinction. Imagine that a father asks an eight-year-old child to go into a bank, point a gun at the teller, and demand money. Who will go to jail? The father is responsible for the child's behavior. He's going to prison while the child will be treated with great leniency by the law. Now imagine that a husband asks his wife to rob the bank. If she is caught, can she plead innocence because her husband told her to rob the bank? Of course not. She will be judged in a manner that reflects her own ability to make good decisions, regardless of what her husband told her to do.

So, What Exactly Is Submission?

Now that we have established what it does *not* mean, let's look at what submission actually means. The word that appears as *submission* in English is a translation of the Greek word *hupotasso*. In the Greek language, this word means "a voluntary attitude of giving in and cooperating."[v]

Submission is the willful posture of using your power to support your husband's leadership. Think of it this way. You can't really say "yes" unless you also have the power to say "no." That means that in order to submit, you recognize your power and you choose to harness it for a greater goal. Instead of dominating or undercutting your husband, you choose to invest in him. The word *submit* was often used in the Greek culture as a military term.[vi] It communicated the idea, once again, of voluntarily placing oneself under the direct leadership of another for the purpose of a higher goal.

Wives are not the only ones who are called to submit in the Bible. Christians are commanded to submit to one another,[vii] to church leaders,[viii] and to government.[ix] In each of these cases, adults willingly recognize another's place of God-given position. You submit to common social customs all the time, even though you have the power and freedom to choose otherwise. When you are flying on an airplane, you don't demand to board first. You wait for your turn. Why? Because you understand that you play a part of maintaining order for the greater good.

Please don't misunderstand submission as the absence of power and influence. Many women believe that they are submitting by adopting the attitude of "Whatever he does is fine. I will just follow along." Then they feel abandoned, violated, and resentful when their husbands make terrible decisions. By choosing submission, a woman does not neglect her influence in her marriage; she actually accentuates it. The more influence she has with her husband, the better. She wants him to know her thoughts, feelings, and opinions. She wants to be his confidante, the one he turns to in good and bad times.

One of the best words to describe the spirit of submission is *empower*.[x] To empower means "to promote the self-actualization or influence of." In essence, a woman empowers her husband when she uses her influence and strength to help him to become a stronger, more confident, and godly person. Instead of threatening his influence, her power actually heightens it.

This is consistent with the fact that God created Eve to be Adam's *ezer* (the word that is usually translated as helper). Read how Dr. Larry Crabb explains the power of an *ezer*, "Notice this: the word *ezer* is never used to refer to a subordinate serving a superior, certainly not when it is used to refer to God as our helper. In the Greek translation of the Old Testament, *ezer* is translated as *boethos*. That word literally means 'help provided by someone strong.'"[xi] Are you getting this? Submission is perhaps the greatest expression of power because it is power harnessed for a greater good.

The opposite of a submissive woman is a dominant or controlling woman. This

> **The opposite of a submissive woman is a dominant or controlling woman. This distinction is made not because one uses her power and the other does not, but rather because each one uses her influence for exactly opposite reasons.**

distinction is made not because one uses her power and the other does not, but rather because each one uses her influence for exactly opposite reasons. The dominant woman cannot trust her husband's leadership. So, she uses all her influence to take his power away from him. She invests all her energy into proving to him that her way is better. Over time, her husband becomes weaker, more insecure, and less invested in meeting his family's needs.

On the flip side, the submissive wife uses all her God-given influence to build her husband's ability to lead. She shares her ideas, opinions, and feelings in a way that builds his confidence and adds to his ability to understand his family's needs. Her goal is not to take his leadership away, but to empower him to grow into this difficult role. She does not use his mistakes to prove his inadequacies, but she succeeds and fails with him. She convinces him that she believes in him and will be by his side. She is able to wait for his leadership, even if she believes that she could do a better job. She tells him daily, through her trust, that she needs him to be a strong and capable leader. Her goal is to convince him that he can trust her with everything he is. The message that her submission communicates is "I know you are not perfect, but I trust in God's work in your life. I believe you are capable of being the great leader for our family that God has called you to be. I will help you with all that I am to achieve this goal."

Over time, the strength that she gives will inevitably empower her husband to grow. The beginning of intimacy is really accepting the *mission* of submission. When a wife embraces the goal of communicating this attitude, it will change the way she views every decision, every conflict, and each interaction with her husband. It is no longer "I win, you lose," but "I can't win unless I am helping you win."

Let's Get Practical

I believe that I am a very strong wife, much stronger than a wife who takes over her marriage. Why? Because my husband trusts and respects me. He listens when I speak and doesn't feel threatened by my power. He knows I will use it for his good. I honestly couldn't say that twenty years ago, but I've made the conscious decision to invest in my husband and marriage over many years. So, how do we take the big picture of submission and translate it into real life?

Each marriage has its own personality. Every couple has certain things they fight about, unique ways of expressing love, and very different life circumstances. But there are some universal principles that can help women interact in a way that will promote growth and intimacy in their marriages.

Submission Means Embracing the Bigger Picture of Marriage

There is a very important distinction between a Christian marriage and one that exists between two people who don't know God. Christians realize that their relationship is about more than the pursuit of happiness. Don't get me wrong. I want to be happy in my marriage! The days and seasons in which marriage is difficult can feel like walking with a bag of sand on my shoulders. But I can endure through those seasons because I know that there is a purpose beyond being blissful soul mates. Marriage is a profound form of revelation.

I've mentioned this in previous chapters, and it's a critical concept to refer back to. Your marriage is painting a picture of God's covenant love, specifically of Christ's love for His bride. This means that your marriage is intended to be something on Earth that reflects spiritual truth. As you work out the practical aspects of navigating life with your husband, you both should be learning about the passionate, committed, and sacrificial love of Jesus. If you don't grab onto this, you won't understand why God created male and female to "fit" together as unique creations. Granted, even Paul admits in Ephesians 5 that this picture is a mystery. We won't fully understand it here on Earth, but we can embrace the fact that there is something very sacred about a Christian marriage.

The differences between your deepest longings and your husband's deepest longings are not the result of social evolution. They reflect the Creator's intention. Author and pastor David Platt put it this way,

> When God made man, then woman, and then brought them together in a relationship called marriage, he wasn't simply rolling the dice, drawing straws, or flipping a coin. He was painting a picture. His intent from the start was to illustrate his love for his people. . . . For God created the marriage relationship to point to a greater reality. From the moment marriage was instituted, God aimed to give the world an illustration of the Gospel.[xii]

When I choose to have a submissive spirit toward my husband, I do so not just because I want a better marriage. When our relationship is in a difficult spot, sub-

I want more than a good marriage. I want a marriage that reflects the goodness of God Himself.

mission matters because I want to be faithful to the picture God is painting in my marriage. I know that my husband cannot become the hero God created him to be if I'm not consistently committing my strength to complete rather than compete with him. I want more than a good marriage. I want a marriage that reflects the goodness of God Himself. When a man and a woman are united in the one-flesh unity of marriage, something of God's goodness is revealed.

Coaches often say, "There is no I in TEAM." In relationships, there is always a place for individuality. For example, good communication begins with sentences that start with "I think…" and "I feel…" However, marriage is made up of two individuals who are joined together for a common journey. Regardless of the outcome, making decisions in the spirit of oneness is vital.

I recently met with a couple who had a conflict about a very difficult decision. After listening to each opinion and perspective, I told them, "What you decide is less important than how you come to that decision. Neither of your perspectives is better than the other's, and things will likely be okay regardless of what you decide. It is the fighting, arguing, and blaming while making the decision that can ultimately create harm." A husband or wife's insistence on getting their own way ruins the picture marriage is meant to paint.

Couples can cope with almost any situation as long as they believe that they are in it together; when it becomes "my opinion versus yours," the blaming starts and oneness stops. There is a time to express individual thoughts, feelings, and preferences; then there is a time to make decisions as a united couple.

Submission is when you recognize that what you are building in your marriage is most often more important than what you disagree about. (Yes, there are definitely exceptions, but they are few.) Have you ever been tempted to remind your husband in hindsight how much better your idea was than his? "If you only would have listened to me!" or "Aren't you glad you took my advice?" This attitude (and trust me, I've been there) is what submission warns us against. Instead, we build intimacy

Submission is when you recognize that what you are building in your marriage is most often more important than what you disagree about.

by focusing on the marriage, not the mistake. "That's okay. We've gotten out of bigger jams!" "We can handle this together." "I'm really glad we decided to do this."

When you insist on getting your way in marriage, you may win the battle but you will lose the war. There are definitely times when a submissive wife stands her ground, confronts her husband, and refuses to follow him. (We will talk about this in the next chapter.) But she does so out of a greater strength from and commitment to God, not just to stay in control.

Submission Means Not Giving Way to Fear

Let's go back to I Peter 3, the passage we looked at earlier in this chapter. Notice this statement, "You are her (Sarah's) daughters if you do what is right and do not give way to fear." The enemy of submission is fear.

I am most likely to use my power destructively when I am afraid. As you learned in the last chapter, marriage makes us vulnerable. It exposes our deepest needs and at times leaves us feeling naked. For a man to be masculine and for a woman to be feminine exposes the greatest level of vulnerability. It means that he must step up (move into the chaos) knowing that he might fail and be humiliated. And it means that she must step back (refuse to control) knowing that she may be disappointed and unprotected.

> I am most likely to use my power destructively when I am afraid.

And so, building intimacy in marriage means that we must confront fear. What if he messes up? What if he leads our family down the wrong path? What if he abandons me or rejects me? When fear wins the day, we are either paralyzed into weakness or mobilized to take control. We either bury our power or use it to bury our husbands.

Let's go back to the real-life examples I mentioned at the beginning of the chapter.

Boundaries with an Angry Husband

Tina's husband, Jim, has a bad temper. He sometimes yells at the children when he is frustrated with them or while he's wrestling with a household project. The kids are obviously hurt by his anger and insensitivity. Should Tina intervene? How can she do this in the spirit of submission?

Tina's husband in this situation is damaging his relationship with their children. She needs to set a boundary with him and help him understand how his temper outbursts impact her and their children and ultimately how they will view him as a father and leader. To do this well, she can't give way to her fear. Maybe Tina doesn't stand up to Jim because she is afraid that he will turn his anger on her. If so, she won't confront him. Or maybe she reacts by "putting him in his place" with an angry outburst of her own. Neither of these fear-based reactions will help him become the father God has called Jim to be.

Tina needs to wait for the right time to have an honest conversation with her husband, so that he's open to listening. She might say something like "I know you easily get frustrated and angry. The way you yell at the kids is a normal reaction. I've done it myself, but it's hurting them and hurting your relationship with them." After listening to Jim's response to this, Tina may want to suggest an idea of how to learn a different way of interacting. Maybe they could sign up for a parenting class at church, listen to a podcast that talks about anger, or meet with a mentor couple for advice. This may be the first of many conversations they have about this.

It's not nagging because she's not telling him what to do. Instead, she is addressing a problem that they need to confront as parents.

Confronting a Job-Hopping Husband

Sam has never been happy at work. Over the course of ten years, he has had nine different jobs and moved his family seven times. Should his wife Laura continue to follow him every time he becomes discontent at work? If she does, is she being submissive or foolish? Should she even tell Sam her objections and concerns? Should she give him an ultimatum?

Laura is understandably exhausted with these disruptive job changes. If her fear gets the best of her, she will either stay silent and swallow her resentment or she will put her foot down: "This is the ninth job in ten years! I'm done. No more moves. No more job-hopping. Either figure out your career or I'm moving on."

Neither of these responses represent the *ezer* Sam desperately needs. Most likely, Sam's pattern of changing jobs is a form of running from failure. While on the surface it might appear that he's chasing his dream, in reality, he doesn't know how to persevere through difficulties like conflict, a demanding boss, or letting people down. Instead, he leaves. As a wise wife, Laura needs to help him see why this pattern isn't helping. Instead of insisting on "no new jobs," she might instead insist that the couple get some counseling to understand the deeper issues.

Protecting Little Eyes

Jamie, Ashley's husband, uses very little discretion when it comes to what his kids watch. He often streams mature content right in front of their young children. Although Ashley is bothered by Jamie's insensitivity, she doesn't know how to put her foot down.

She's mentioned it a few times, but he always dismisses her. She has read about the importance of having a "submissive and quiet spirit." What should she do?

Ashley has a legitimate concern that she needs to voice. Again, fear will play a role here. To confront Jamie appropriately, Ashley can't give in to the fear that Jamie's behaviors trigger in her. If she does, she will probably act more like a mother scolding him than a wife asking him to step up to be the hero.

In this situation, Ashley needs to set the stage for a conflict. She's already brought up the concern in the past and Jamie didn't respond, so this interaction has to be more direct. It might go something like this, "Jamie, I know I've shared this with you before, but I need to bring it up again because it really troubles me. Our kids are very impressionable. You probably don't even notice them in the room sometimes, but they see and hear really raw things. I'm not okay with that. It's not fair for you to ask or expect me to keep them out of the family room because of what you are watching. Something needs to change."

Your fear will always play a role in how you negotiate situations like these within your marriage. Bossy, dominant wives are just as fearful as mousy, quiet wives. They just handle their fear differently. One takes over and the other one retreats. Submission doesn't do either of those things. Submission means submitting your fears to God, trusting in Him to give you the strength to be the wise woman who builds her house.

Seeing the "bigger picture" of my marriage helps me realize that fear doesn't have to dominate me. While I work on trusting my imperfect husband, I am also working to more completely trust my perfect Husband. This needs to be more about my yielding to His ways rather than yielding to what my husband wants. Yes, the vulnerability of marriage can be frightening and intimidating, but it is much less so when I refuse to stake my survival on how my husband reacts to me.

I love how Larry Crabb explains it, "A woman with a gentle spirit does not live in mortal fear of her husband. Fear no longer requires her to protect her soul. She is therefore free to honor a higher good, to respect her husband as a fellow image-bearer, and to invite him by her gentle attitude to be the man he was created to be."[xiii]

If you are committed to building intimacy in your marriage, trust the One who created it in the first place. There is no new secret to a happy marriage that overrides how God designed us to interact as husband and wife. You have power. That power is building or tearing down intimacy in your marriage. God has given you wisdom on how to use your power in a way that honors Him and promotes intimacy.

That being said, we live in a very fallen world. Each of us brings baggage and wounds into marriage. Even young couples have been married long enough to have reinforced the need to self-protect. How does God's ideal of submission filter through the pain and legitimate fear of real-life marriage? In the next two chapters, we will address what happens when we retreat or take over in fear.

Endnotes

i See Matthew 25:14–30.

ii See Genesis 1:26–28.

iii See Genesis 16 and 21.

iv Genesis 21:12.

v https://www.biblestudytools.com/lexicons/greek/nas/hupotasso.html.

vi https://www.biblestudytools.com/lexicons/greek/nas/hupotasso.html.

vii I Corinthians 16:15 and Ephesians 5:2.

viii Hebrews 2:13.

ix Romans 13:1 and I Peter 2:13.

x https://www.merriam-webster.com/dictionary/empower.

xi Larry Crabb, *Fully Alive: A Biblical Vision of Gender That Frees Men and Women to Live Beyond Stereotypes* (MI: Baker Books, 2013), p. 52.

xii David Platt, *Counter Culture* (Carol Stream, IL: Tyndale, 2017), 138.

xiii *Fully Alive*, p. 61.

Chapter 5

a time to stand up

If you followed her on social media, you might envy Jillian. With three beautiful young children and a successful husband, Jillian always looks put together on the inside and out. She's that friend who is quick with an encouraging word or a reminder to trust in God. You would never know that behind those smiling eyes and stylish haircut is a woman in deep pain. Her marriage may look like a romance story with fun vacations and romantic photo ops, but her reality tells a different story.

When Jillian reached out to me, she described what living with her husband, Brandon, was really like. Their marriage didn't begin this way. Jillian initially loved how boldly Brandon made decisions, but over the years, his decisiveness slid into control. With each passing day, her husband had somehow become "stronger" as Jillian became a silent bystander in her own home. With small children to care for, losing the confidence and recognition she once got from work made her feel even more trapped in an unhappy marriage. Her talents and skills, which at one time had flourished, withered without the warm rays of freedom and encouragement. Now, Jillian felt like a prisoner who obeyed orders and suppressed opinions to keep the peace. The few times she tried to stand up for herself resulted in Brandon becoming defensive and accusing her of selfishness. She knew that her children were suffering, too. As much as she tried to encourage them, the harsh words spoken by their father left irreparable damage.

Jillian thought of leaving him, but there was also so much good to their marriage. *He's such a great provider. There are weeks and even months where we all get along pretty well. It wasn't always like this. The kids need their father, even if he's not a perfect one.*

Where can a woman like Jillian begin finding the hero in a husband like this?

How Did We Get Here?

Maybe as you're reading, you see yourself in Jillian. Most people who know you wouldn't describe you as weak, but they don't see what happens behind the closed doors of your marriage. No one knows how difficult it is for you to assert yourself or set a boundary. You may wonder, *How did I get myself into this situation?*

Early in every marriage, a man and a woman jockey for position. They don't know they are doing it, but their decisions and conflicts are not just about what color to paint the walls but about who is going to be in control. This isn't a bad thing; it's just the reality of how an intimate relationship forms. They subconsciously work to establish a "dance" of whose opinion will matter the most and how they will approach their inevitable disagreements.

I vividly remember some of the first conflicts of my marriage. One was about an extension cord. We went to the hardware store to buy one for the lights we wanted to put on our porch. Mike picked out a sturdy fifteen-foot outdoor extension cord that cost about twenty-five dollars. I found a six-foot indoor/outdoor version that cost five dollars. I argued with him about how we could save fifteen dollars if we bought two of the cheaper versions.

We have had this same argument hundreds of times over during our decades of marriage. In fact, we just had it again yesterday over a puzzle board. This plays out every time we buy a car, washing machine, or plan a vacation.

Yes, we have fundamentally different views on how to spend money, but the argument that we first had in that hardware store was different. It wasn't just about what extension cord to buy or even how we would spend money as a couple. It was about power. Who would get their way in marriage?

When Jillian and Brandon first had disagreements like this, Jillian always yielded. Brandon didn't ask for her input and dismissed her whenever she disagreed with him on little things. By constantly yielding, Jillian didn't use her power to equip and challenge Brandon. Instead, she gave in to his every idea and decision. While she thought she was being a supportive wife, she inadvertently contributed to the wrong "dance" in their relationship, one where Brandon has all the power.

No husband will be a hero if he owns all the power in marriage.

No husband will be a hero if he owns all the power in marriage. He needs his wife's input, encouragement, support, and accountability. Without it, he will alienate his children, make unwise decisions, and lose his wife's respect. The more inadequate he feels, the more controlling he will become, masking his fear with a take-charge attitude that usually results in unquestioned intimidation. His wife, fearing his anger, becomes more passive. It's a dangerous cycle to fall into.

Sometimes this happens because of the ways we've learned to relate to people early in life. Although living with a controlling husband is stifling, for some women it can feel strangely familiar. Maybe you grew up in a family where you had no voice. Your mom or dad made your decisions, convincing you that you couldn't make them for yourself. Dating and marrying a powerful man initially felt like a great fit because it's all that you've known.

Even a strong woman may have aspects of marriage in which she fails to use her power when needed. At times, I've found myself afraid to use my power appropriately in marriage because I hate conflict. I love to make people happy and try to never disappoint them. And honestly, it's easier to go with the flow than to have a tense conversation. Over the years, it's been difficult for me to not give in to fear when I know I need to confront. It often feels safer in the short run to keep my mouth shut than to intentionally walk into conflict. Looking back on my marriage, there are times when I wish I'd had the courage to stand up and use my power more effectively for my husband's good.

Submission should never be used as an excuse to hide from the influence and responsibility that women have within marriage.

This pattern can be reinforced for Christian women when we misunderstand biblical roles in marriage. In the previous chapter, we talked about the importance of submission. Submission does not mean that you become weak. In fact, it takes great courage and self-control to be the woman God has called you to be in your marriage. Submission should never be used as an excuse to hide from the influence and responsibility that women have within marriage.

There is a vast and distinct difference between a woman who is appropriately submissive and a woman who is weak. This difference is communicated through two words: *empower* and *enable*. Both of these words speak to what we do with our power.

When a wife *empowers* her husband, it means that all her strength is behind him, encouraging and helping. In contrast, weakness leads to a woman who *enables* her husband, standing silently by as he does whatever he thinks is right. She withdraws her power instead of backing him with strength, accountability, and encouragement toward the right things.

Any wife can fall into this pattern out of exhaustion, feeling helpless, bitterness, or the momentum of the "dance" she and her husband established early on. As you learned in previous chapters, this might be a "workable" marriage, but it certainly won't be an intimate one.

When to Stand Your Ground

Perhaps the most difficult question I have ever wrestled with in my own marriage and as I've counseled others is *how do you know when to stand up?* How do I know when this is a "hill worth dying on" versus just thinking my own way is right all the time?

The best place to start in sorting this out is to go right back to God's Word. Here are the Scripture references that address a Christian wife's role in marriage:

Wives, submit to your husbands as to the Lord. For the husband is the head of the wife as Christ is the head of the church, his body, of which He is the Savior. Now as the church submits to Christ, so also wives should submit to their husbands in everything. (Eph. 5:22–24 NIV)

Wives, submit to your husbands, as is fitting in the Lord. (Col. 3:18 NIV)

Wives, in the same way be submissive to your husbands so that, if any of them do not believe the word, they may be won over without words by the behavior of their wives, when they see the purity and reverence of your lives. (I Peter 3:1, 2 NIV)

If you read these passages in context, you will see that right next to each teaching on how a woman should relate to her husband is a command instructing a husband on how to treat his wife. Invariably, the Bible tells a husband to love and cherish his wife. If a husband is faithful to his role, submission in a Christian marriage is safe because a wife's interests and opinions will be valued. It would not be that hard to submit to a husband who acted like Jesus! Unfortunately, a wife's submission does not appear to be necessary only when her husband is being a hero.

The first passage listed here, Ephesians 5:24, says that a wife should submit to her husband "in everything." Does this really mean in *everything*? Doesn't that set up men to be dominant misogynists? The command to submit in everything seems to run totally against a loving God who wants to protect us from harmful and hard-hearted leadership. Would He really want an abused wife to stay in a relationship in which she was daily assaulted by her husband? Would He want children to continue to be sexually molested by their father as their mother clings to the role of submission?

Unfortunately, we don't have a recorded question and answer session with Jesus or the apostle Paul to directly answer questions like these. To make matters even more complicated, the Bible was written in a different cultural context than our present day. But we do have within the Bible consistent principles that help us wisely sort through such practical questions.

Let's begin with the fact that no submission is absolute, apart from submitting to God Himself. Each of the three Scriptures noted above also uses an important qualifier to the command of submission. Ephesians 5 says to submit "as to the Lord." Likewise, Colossians 3:18 says to submit "as is fitting to the Lord." In I Peter 3:6, Peter continues his discussion of submission telling women to "do what is right." God has placed husbands in a position of leadership within marriage. Wives respect their husbands out of reverence and obedience to God. It is not a husband's authority that ultimately rules, but God's.

When we apply this principle, it gives us at least three reasons why it is absolutely critical that you go beyond supporting your husband and use your power to draw a needed boundary as the partner God created you to be.

Don't Join Him in Sin

You know right from wrong, but what if your husband has a fuzzier definition of morality. A little white lie never hurt anyone. Some pornography could spice up our sex life. Everyone fudges a little on their taxes.

Whenever a Christian is called to submit to any human authority (boss, husband, pastor, government, and so on), God is recognized as the larger authority. This means that when God's law is in conflict with a human authority, a Christian submits to God rather than man. This doesn't mean that your husband has to be perfectly righteous for you to respect his leadership. He doesn't even have to be a Christian. But if he is asking you to participate in something you know is wrong, obey God.

A few years ago, we were taking a road trip from our home in Colorado Springs to our favorite little town in the mountains. I was driving because I like to drive and I get carsick in the mountains. We hit a long stretch of a flat two-lane highway. Having made this drive many times, we knew that this would be about fifteen miles of straight, clear road. Mike (who likes to drive faster than I do) urged me to step on the gas, "Come on, Baby, this is where you can make up some time." The speed limit was sixty-five and I was already going over seventy. After a few husbandly prompts, I reluctantly sped up to about seventy-eight. Sure enough, a police car passed going the other way and abruptly turned around. As we pulled over, I was fuming at Mike. Before I could say anything, he apologized, "I'm sorry. I know I was pushing you to go faster. I'll talk to the cop." And he did.

Mike explained that he told me to speed up. "So, should I give you the ticket?" the police officer asked my husband. "Yes, I'll take it," Mike replied. The police officer went back to his cruiser while we waited with the tension. When he came back, the officer told me, "I'm letting you off with a warning. But next time, please don't listen to your husband."

Marriage roles do not cancel out our first responsibility to love and obey God's commands. I definitely think there are times when God would say to a wise wife, "Please don't listen to your husband."

Marriage roles do not cancel out our first responsibility to love and obey God's commands.

I think He would have said this to a woman named Sapphira.

Acts 5 tells the story of this wife who was a coconspirator with Ananias, her husband, in sin. They sold a piece of land and promised to give the proceeds to the church but secretly decided to hold some of the money back. Although there was nothing wrong with keeping some of the money, they lied to their church. When their pastor, Peter, found out he confronted them individually. First, Ananias told Peter that they had donated the full amount to the church. God killed Ananias on the spot.

About three hours later, Sapphira came to Peter. She had no idea what had just happened to her husband. Peter asked her, "Tell me, is this the price you and Ananias got for the land?" And she said, "Yes, that is the price" (Acts 5:8 NIV). Sapphira was then delivered the same fate that her husband had just faced.

In this story, God dealt equally with this husband and wife. They made the decision to sin together, and each was given the opportunity to come clean. Sapphira was punished harshly for her sin, even though she may have been acting in "submission" to her husband.

In Romans 13 Paul writes about submitting to the government, "there is no authority except that which God has established" (Rom. 13:1 NIV). God gives a husband's authority to him and he is under God's authority. When a husband asks his wife to do something that is clearly sinful, God vetoes the husband's authority.

There are lots of different examples of how this might play out, some obvious and some more subtle. If your husband asks you to be in an open marriage, don't do it. If he tells you to lie, say no. If he won't let you go to church or honor your parents, his leadership has gone out of bounds of God's authority. In both big and little things, we want to honor and obey God above keeping our husbands happy.

Don't Be a Silent Party to Sin

Marriage is the union between two sinners. That means that your husband will not only sin but has a river of selfishness, pride, and rebellion coursing through his heart. And so do you. In Romans, Paul teaches us that the only difference between a Christian and non-Christian is that the Holy Spirit gives Christians the power to not be slaves to all the wrong thoughts and motives that threaten to overtake us.[i] The battle of sin is a reality in every marriage.

It's not your job as a wife to keep your husband from sinning. If you're honest, you'll admit that you have a full-time job surrendering your own heart to the Lord. But it is your responsibility as your husband's wife, friend, and sister in Christ to confront a pattern of sin in his life (and he has the same responsibility to you).

As you learned in Chapter 2, you have a lot of influence with your husband. He looks to you for support and approval in whatever he is doing. Don't use your power to encourage or cover up for something that is destructive in your husband's life.

The classic example of this is a man who has a substance addiction. If a guy is using, his wife will know about it. Even if she thinks his substance abuse is a problem, in some ways she might be silently supporting it. Maybe because of her own shame, she looks the other way and helps keep his using a secret. She covers for him when he cannot make it to work, makes excuses for him with his friends and family, and compensates for his irregular behavior. She might even do this with the intention of being a supportive wife. For their marriage to heal, she has to confront his addiction and stop playing a contributing role in his destructive pattern.

Sin has serious emotional, spiritual, and physical consequences. Those consequences are not just for the sinner but also for those related to him. The impact of sexual abuse, for example, is felt by anyone involved with the perpetrator.

> There is nothing godly or submissive about looking the other way when your husband is choosing a pattern of sin.

There is nothing godly or submissive about looking the other way when your husband is choosing a pattern of sin. You're not his judge, condemning him, but you are called to be a caring friend refusing to stand by while he destroys himself.

Some sin patterns (like stealing, lying, having an affair) are obviously destructive and require you to do more than just say something. Standing up may mean leaving a man who refuses to get help for sinful and destructive patterns.

My friend, Jonathan Daugherty, tells the story of how his wife gave him a great gift. She left him. As a Christian man, everything looked good on the outside, but he had a secret addiction to pornography that led to random hookups. A few years into their marriage, Jonathan confessed his addiction to his wife, Elaine. She was understandably shocked and devastated. Jonathan felt unburdened for the first time in his life. He no longer had to carry his secret. But a few weeks later, he found himself in a hotel room with a woman he'd met online. He came home to his wife's bags packed and the message, "I never want to see you again!"

Jonathan shares about the power of that moment.

> I never truly believed Elaine would leave me. It's true. Even as I was engaging in multiple affairs, lying daily to her, and becoming increasingly more difficult to live with, I never thought she would pack up and leave. But now I stood in the doorway of our house, watching her car fade away down the street, and I believed...Elaine leaving was just what I needed to bring me to the end of myself, truly to that place of rock bottom. And leaving with her were my delusions of continuing a double life.[ii]

I know marriages, like Jonathan's, that have survived infidelity, addictions, abuse, and much more. But the road to healing has required telling the truth and drawing a line in the sand. For some it has involved physical separation and years of intensive counseling. Your marriage will not get better by ignoring what's wrong with it. Proverbs says, "Faithful are the wounds of a friend." Do you love your husband enough to humbly wound him if necessary? Are you willing to disrupt the status quo for the sake of your family?

Other sin issues are less obvious. For example, when you do say something about your husband's patterns of greed, off-color jokes, occasional use of recreational drugs, or white lies? Don't we have our own pockets of "acceptable sins?" This is why pursuing God's forgiveness and wisdom is so critical to becoming a wife who is truly a blessing to her husband. As the Bible says, first we address the plank in our own eyes and then we will see clearly to lovingly and humbly helping our husband see how God invites him to grow.

Confront Destructive Dynamics

A thirty-eight-year-old woman named Alexandra came to me for help with her troubled marriage. At first, she was vague about the problems she was having. She talked about feeling depressed and anxious all the time. She downplayed the troubles in her marriage, saying that her husband was basically a good guy who sometimes made mistakes. After a few meetings, she began to share the fear that she felt at home. In fits of rage, he screamed the vilest words at her and threatened her with physical violence.

Deep down, Alexandra felt responsible for the problems in her marriage. She tried desperately to please him to keep him from exploding. Her husband explained his behavior by putting it back on her, "If you wouldn't have given me that snarky look, I wouldn't have gotten so mad!" Alexandra bought the lie that somehow, she deserved this treatment. Every fiber of her being seemed to fight the realization that she was in an abusive and dangerous marriage.

There are women like Alexandra, who quietly endure living with threatening men. Others are in lesser versions of harmful marriage dynamics. Mental illness like clinical depression, bipolar disorder, and addictions can turn even a loving husband into a man who becomes hurtful to himself and those around him. It is often difficult to know where to draw the line when you're in the middle of the mess. You may feel too afraid, embarrassed, or isolated to seek help.

Men and women are separate from all creation in that they were created in God's image. Their souls are eternal, they are able to make moral decisions and they are deeply sensitive to interactions with others. Based on the value that God has given to humans, we are commanded to treat one another with love and kindness.[iii] Regardless of age, wealth, race, gender, or position in society, this status as an image-bearer of God makes each person precious.

Destructive dynamics within your home need to be confronted. It's not enough to say "I'm sorry" or "That's the way my parents fought." Yes, those are reasons. We all bring baggage into marriage, including our own sinful tendencies. But a reason is not an excuse. As husband and wife, we must insist on treating each other with dignity.

My friend Gary Thomas wrote one of the most respected Christian books on marriage in my generation, The *Sacred Marriage*. In this book, Gary makes the argument that God created marriage for our holiness, not just for our happiness. He encourages husbands and wives to endure through hard times and disappointments because of the sacred nature of their covenant with each other. After years of traveling the world, speaking on this message, Gary was grieved at how his book about the importance of marriage has been used to justify incredibly damaging patterns in marriage.

This great champion of marriage, even difficult marriages, wrote a blog lamenting the horrible ways the Bible has been used to enslave women. Gary concludes:

> *How does it honor the concept of "Christian marriage" to enforce the continuance of an abusive, destructive relationship that is slowly squeezing all life and joy out of a woman's soul? Our focus has to be on urging men to love their wives like Christ loves the church, not on telling women to put up with husbands mistreating their wives like Satan mistreats us. We should confront and stop the work of Satan, not enable it.*[iv]

God has given you power, even if you are in a marriage in which you feel powerless. One purpose of that power is to stand in the way of injustice. Proverbs 31:25 describes an excellent wife as "clothed with strength and dignity." This strength and dignity is not a brash insistence on getting her way but an inner confidence that confronts injustice. No husband has the right to treat his wife or children in a way that degrades or humiliates them. By doing this, he is robbing them of the worth and dignity with which they were created.

God has given you power, even if you are in a marriage in which you feel powerless. One purpose of that power is to stand in the way of injustice.

There are other times when, because of emotional pain or mental illness, a man becomes destructive and dangerous to himself. Kelsey's husband, Kevin, was a rock-star executive who quickly climbed the ladder of success in his company. An athlete, Christian leader, and great father, he seemed to be the envy of every other man. One day, Kevin couldn't get out of bed. He had a splitting headache and felt like his entire body was on fire. That was the beginning of a downward spiral that would include panic attacks and debilitating depression. Six months later, Kelsey's hero was actively suicidal and using pain medication just to get through the day. Kevin was too embarrassed to let anyone know what he was going through or to seek professional help. It was time for Kelsey to step up and get Kevin the help and support he himself couldn't reach out for.

There are many different levels of dysfunction within marriages. Husbands and wives in the heat of an argument may say things they deeply regret. Controlling and manipulative strategies in marriage may, at some level, qualify as "emotional abuse." Unfortunately, living in the close confines of marriage means that we are bound to hurt one another. Those destructive dynamics need to be confronted for a marriage to thrive, but domestic violence or other forms of blatant abuse require immediate intervention and separation.

If you live in a destructive relationship, I implore you to seek wisdom and help. Please resist the temptation to misuse biblical concepts like submission, humility, or forgiveness to justify a sinful and destructive pattern in a relationship. While the Bible is clear that we are always to forgive people who harm us, forgiveness doesn't necessarily mean that we go back to relating as if nothing ever happened. A severe offense or a pattern of abusive behavior breaks trust, and a relationship can't be close unless trust is rebuilt.

How to Stand Your Ground

Check Your Spirit

"Juli, I knew it was wrong, but I was just so angry!" Through tears, Laura confessed that she had slept with another man. "I just wanted him to feel the pain I felt. I don't want to be the victim anymore."

Laura's story reminded me of the warning Paul gives us all when confronting a friend or brother in sin.

> Brothers and sisters, if someone is caught in a sin, you who live by the Spirit should restore that person gently. But watch yourselves, or you also may be tempted. Carry each other's burdens, and in this way, you will fulfill the law of Christ. If anyone thinks they are something when they are not, they deceive themselves. Each one should test their own actions. Then they can take pride in themselves alone, without comparing themselves to someone else, for each one should carry their own load. (Gal. 6:1–4)

Whenever the Bible tells us to confront someone we love, we are reminded to first examine our own hearts and to stay in a posture of humility. If you've gotten this far in the chapter, there's a good chance you've connected with what I've written. You can see that you need to stand against a weakness or sin pattern in your husband's life. Please be careful. Ask the Lord to search your heart and to show you where you have contributed to the problem with your own weakness or sin.

Whenever the Bible tells us to confront someone we love, we are reminded to first examine our own hearts and to stay in a posture of humility.

Satan may take the opportunity of your husband's failings to make you feel justified in your own sin patterns. I've been there. I've spent time in the cycle of blaming and shaming my husband in my self-righteousness. God has shown me how at times I've closed my heart to my husband with bitterness and unforgiveness.

When it's time to stand up to your husband, that doesn't mean submission goes out the window. We are always called to submit to God who tells us,

> Therefore, as God's chosen people, holy and dearly loved, clothe yourselves with compassion, kindness, humility, gentleness and patience. Bear with each other and forgive one another if any of you has a grievance against someone. Forgive as the Lord forgave you. And over all these virtues put on love, which binds them all together in perfect unity. (Col. 3:12–14)

Even while you're "standing your ground," God wants to clothe your spirit with compassion, kindness, humility, gentleness, and patience. Yes, there is a reason for righteous anger and a time to set clear boundaries. But your anger can quickly turn into pride, revenge, and a hard heart. Remember, submission isn't about whether or not your mouth is moving but about the posture of your heart toward God. If you exchange insult for insult, wound for wound, and punish your husband for his bitterness, are you not falling into the same thing you're judging him for?

Reach Out for Help

The kind of pain described in this chapter will make you want to hide. You'll convince yourself that you can handle this on your own. You'll minimize and rationalize, telling yourself that things will eventually get better on their own. My friend, they won't. You need help.

Several years ago, I was walking through a very painful season.

One day sitting in our bedroom, I was pouring out my heart to Mike. Through sobs I told him how crushed and alone I felt. He then asked me, "If someone with this situation came to you for counseling, what would you tell her? You have all this training and you help so many people through tough situations. Put on your psychologist hat and counsel yourself." Although he was well-meaning, his words felt like salt in a wound.

Being my own psychologist is impossible. When I'm the one in pain, I lose all perspective. Mike and I have gone to marriage counseling during many different seasons of life. Yes, I feel strange in the waiting room, especially when one of my books is sitting there on the coffee table. But I need help as much as anyone. I need my friends and mentors to call me on my stuff, to give me wisdom when I don't know where to turn, and to hug me when I'm hurting. And so do you.

Pain makes all of us feel untethered. We just want it to go away. We find ourselves saying yes when we should say no. We hold on to anger that poisons us. We blame ourselves for things we have no control over. We believe the enemy when he shouts, "You'll never get out of this!"

God made us for community. Marriage was never intended to be an island for two people to bury all their secrets from the rest of the world. The more dysfunctional your marriage gets, the more likely you will be to isolate. A controlling husband will feel threatened if you have other people in your life, and you may want to minimize what's happening because of shame and fear.

If your marriage is in a destructive cycle, if either you or your husband is battling addiction or mental illness, please don't try to address these issues without help. An unstable marriage can quickly escalate if you try to confront problems without support around you. Even with the best of intentions, you're likely to get flustered the next time your husband falls into the familiar destructive patterns of your marriage. A wise counselor and encouraging mentor can help you set healthy boundaries and hold you accountable to follow through on those boundaries.

Address the Problem; Then Let God Fight for You

While this book is about your tremendous power in your marriage, I want to remind you that power does not mean control. You cannot argue, convince, or manipulate your husband out of sin or brokenness. We often try to change our husbands' wrong behavior by nagging: "Don't you think you've had enough to drink?" "I've asked you a hundred times not to treat people that way!" "I wish you would stop swearing in front of the kids!" This strategy has been proven over the centuries to do one thing: backfire. The more a woman nags, the less a man listens. If a man is addicted to pornography, the last thing that will motivate him to stop is his wife's constant shaming. It would be humiliating for him to change his life just because she told him to. He may even become more involved in it to prove to his wife that she cannot control him. You will never influence your husband by becoming his mom. Mothers tell their sons what to do, basically suppressing masculinity. A wise wife calls her husband to something greater, inviting masculinity, and then lets him battle with God, not with her.

> A wise wife calls her husband to something greater, inviting masculinity, and then lets him battle with God, not with her.

Confront the problem, set the boundary, and then get out of God's way. Let's apply this to Jillian's situation at the beginning of the chapter. Before she says a word to Brandon, she needs to ask the Lord to search her own heart. She needs the care and wisdom of a counselor (which is how I met her). And then she needs to speak (or write in a letter) something like this:

> *Brandon, over the last few years, our marriage has become a very stressful environment. I know you have a lot of pressure at work, but I feel like I'm walking on eggshells with you much of the time. Neither of us want this for us or for our kids. I'm seeking help from a counselor and I'm asking you to go to counseling with me.*
>
> *You don't have to answer now, but I need you to consider it.*
>
> *Some things need to change for me, for you, and for our children to be healthy. I want you to be part of that change.*
>
> *I love you and I'm asking God to show us how to fight for us.*

When a woman uses her influence this way, her husband realizes that he has to make his own decision. She's decided that she wants to learn to be healthy, but she can't force him to make that same decision. She takes herself out of the equation. He becomes more aware of the consequences of whatever he chooses. He's responsible for his choices, and she is responsible for hers.

Remember that the battle for your marriage is often a battle of fear, even for your husband. Men don't become dominating, insensitive, and abusive because they are confident. They become that way when they are afraid...afraid of appearing weak, of being exposed or of failing. Just as you have to surrender *your* fear to the Lord, so does your husband. It is His battle to win.

I love the story of the battle recorded in 2 Chronicles 20. King Jehoshaphat was surrounded by a massive, overwhelming army. Through a prophet, God said to the king and his warriors:

King Jehoshaphat, listen! All you who live in Judah and Jerusalem, listen! The Lord says to you, "Do not be afraid. Do not lose hope because of this huge army. The battle is not yours. It is God's . . . You will not have to fight this battle. Take your positions. Stand firm. You will see how the Lord will save you. Judah and Jerusalem, do not be afraid. Do not lose hope. Go out and face them tomorrow. The Lord will be with you."

I'm not suggesting that your husband is the enemy that God will defeat, but there is a spiritual battle for your marriage. You fight it by trusting God, standing firm, and remembering that God is with you.

My friend, even if in this season of your marriage you feel very powerless, God has given you influence—not to change your husband, but to be a force of good in his life. *Every wife will make a difference in her husband's life, even through her refusal to use her power.* This means that every wife must choose whether she will use her influence to build her house or to tear it down.

Endnotes

i See Romans 6.

ii Jonathan Daugherty, *Secrets* (London, England: Tate Publishing, 2009), 132.

iii I Peter 3:8.

iv https://garythomas.com/2016/11/29/enough-enough/

Chapter 6

a wife's greatest dilemma

There is no question that our current culture encourages the trend of strong women and passive men. TV shows and movies almost without exception present the woman as having it all together while the guy is still trying to figure life out. He's the butt of the joke, helpless to stand up to his competent, capable wife. Some examples of this include this quote by author Kathy Lette who said, "Why do men like intelligent women? Because opposites attract," and another anonymous quote I've heard is, "A man may be a fool and not know it, but not if he's married." Christian husbands can relate to laugh lines like "happy wife, happy life," essentially adopting a "Yes, Dear" approach to disagreements to keep the peace.

Author Margo Kaufman once wrote, "The only thing worse than a man you can't control is a man you can."[i] I've experienced this bind. Have you? I desperately want to build the hero in my husband. I want to see his strength, but I find myself too afraid and too proud to trust him.

While women jockey to be in charge, we often hate where it leads us in marriage. I was recently talking with a friend in her late forties who honestly shared, "I'm just tired! I don't want to do this anymore. The kids ask me for everything. They never go to their dad. Even when he tries to help them, they brush him off. Why do I have to carry all the stress of our home, solve every crisis while trying to manage my own life?"

Every marriage has a power balance between a man and woman. In the last chapter, we looked at how destructive a powerful husband and weak wife can be, but the opposite is also true. Intimacy in marriage means that both the husband and wife assume their God-given power and use it to build rather than tear down.

Why Women Take Over

If men want to be a hero and women want to be married to a hero, then why can't they just make that happen? Why do we find ourselves sabotaging the very strength we hope to see in our husbands? Here are a few reasons why.

We Are Cursed

While this cultural moment is no champion of marriage by God's design, the tension of women taking over is definitely not a new one. We can look way back to how marriage first went wrong in the Garden of Eden. Dr. Larry Crabb wrote a book called *The Silence of Adam* in which he asks the question, where was Adam when his wife was first deceived by the serpent? Adam's passivity was as great a problem as Eve's infamous bite. When God confronted the couple in Genesis 3, Adam blamed his wife rather than taking responsibility for his own lack of initiative and integrity.

We can see in Genesis 3:16 that the fall resulted in a disordered relationship between every husband and wife. God said to the woman, "Your desire will be for your husband, but he will rule over you." Instead of co-reigning together to subdue the earth, a husband and his wife would now wrestle continually with the tension of wanting to subdue each other.

At the risk of sounding dramatic, the power struggle so common in marriage is demonic. God's enemy, Satan, will aim to destroy everything God made as holy and perfect. Your marriage is no exception. The last thing Satan wants is for you and your husband to experience the perfection of interacting as God designed a husband and wife to love each other.

Our own sinfulness is the often-unconscious decision to collude with Satan against God's design rather than trusting Him to lead us into the fulfillment of that design. And so, along with the first wife, we experience the tension of longing for our husband to be a hero while also wanting to dismantle his power. We place our husbands in a diabolical double bind, saying to them, "I want you to lead but to lead the way I tell you to lead."

We Are Afraid

As you learned earlier in this book, God's design for marriage exposes both a man's and a woman's deepest fears. To complicate matters further, most men enter into marriage feeling ill equipped to face the challenges of intimacy, spiritual leadership, and providing for a family. While marriage asks a man to step into the role of hero, he often lacks the skills and mentors that can guide him into becoming one. What does it look like to be a good husband? Father? Where are the role models for men to follow? No man

> We place our husbands in a diabolical double bind, saying to them, "I want you to lead but to lead the way I tell you to lead."

wants to attempt something new if he doesn't have a road map to success. As one young man recently told me, "Better to play it safe." Does this give him an excuse for his lack of engagement and responsibility? No, but it may help you understand why he's not "manning up."

Honestly, both men and women are safer in marriage if she takes control of the relationship. He doesn't have to fear failure, and she doesn't have to fear being let down. A lot of men and women just agree to build their relationship this way. It's not like they talked about it, but if they had been so brutally honest, the conversation may have gone like this:

> **Woman:** *I'd really like to see you take some ownership and responsibility for our marriage.*
>
> **Man:** *No, you wouldn't. The few times I've tried to step up, you quickly let me know how I'm not doing things the way you think I should. It's never good enough for you, so I'll just let you have it your way.*
>
> **Woman:** *Well, you should know how to do things right. If I wait around for you to figure this out, our family, our finances, and my heart will be a mess. I feel a lot better just taking care of things myself.*
>
> **Man:** *Fine with me! I have plenty of other things I'd rather spend my energy on.*

And so, they settle into an unspoken truce that keeps them both safe but nowhere close to intimate. Can you relate?

We Are Immature

"How many children do you have?" Women are known to humorously reply to this question, "Four, including my husband."

Now just imagine for a moment that a man answered the question this way, including his wife among the children in the home. Why is it funny for a wife to refer to her husband as a child but unthinkable for a man to tell this same joke?

Women justify a marriage takeover when their husbands have proven that they either don't want to or can't handle the responsibility. She slides into "mom" mode, complaining how she is married to an adolescent. Addressing this problem in your marriage begins by acknowledging that your husband isn't the only one who needs to grow up. Yes, you can point to a hundred ways that you may be more responsible and mature than he is. While your frustration may be justified, it also probably unveils your own immaturity. I know because I've been there.

When Mike and I got married, I appeared on the surface to be more mature than he was. I was goal oriented, knew what I wanted from life, and had been a Christian far longer than my husband. As much as I loved Mike's laid-back approach to life when we were dating, I wasn't such a fan once we were married. I complained about always having to be the serious one—the responsible one.

I remember one incident that represented the early years of our marriage. Mike and I lived in a two-story townhouse. We agreed that we would clean the house together on Saturdays—he would clean the upstairs, and I would clean the downstairs. Along came Saturday. After breakfast, I grabbed the cleaning supplies and tackled my part of the house. Mike turned on the TV. Long after I had finished my part of the house, Mike decided to go for a run, and then lunch, and then a nap. As the hours wore on, I got more and more angry. By about 9:00 PM, I self-righteously grabbed the cleaning supplies and began working on the upstairs. I'm sure I sighed loudly and slammed cupboards, letting my new husband know what a martyr he had married. I was so mad at my husband that I slept on the couch that night. I really lost it when Mike came downstairs the next morning, chuckled at me sprawled on the couch, and said, "Well, I got a good night's sleep!"

In the weeks and months that followed, Mike and I hashed out this ongoing issue so perfectly displayed by the cleaning episode. I learned that my husband wasn't the only one who needed to grow up. I could be controlling and manipulative in my expectations, sparking my husband to respond with passive-aggressive stubbornness.

I may have been subtler in how I demanded my way, but I was really acting no more grown-up than Mike was. I saw myself as taking the high road by proving to Mike and myself how much more responsible I was than he. True maturity would have been to confront the issue with honesty and a willingness to understand what was going on inside my husband's heart.

Truth be told, we all have a bratty, selfish, sinful kid inside us.

A wife's greatest dilemma is that you don't want to be the leader in your marriage, but you also don't want to be led. Using your power to take control feels safe, but it also builds a barrier to intimacy. Without even realizing it, you've likely built coping strategies to keep yourself from feeling vulnerable in your marriage.

> A wife's greatest dilemma is that you don't want to be the leader in your marriage, but you also don't want to be led.

When I wrote the first version of this book (way back in the dark ages), no Christian woman would have wanted to admit to being bossy. Although not quite a badge of honor, a lot of wives will now readily acknowledge being the one in charge. Just listen to a group of wives complaining about their lazy or clueless husbands. They egg one another on with advice on how to put a man in his place.

How Women Take Over

Take-charge wives use different strategies to keep the upper hand of power in the relationship. Here are a few of them:

Bethany Bossypants

In some marriages, there is no question who runs the relationship. Within twenty minutes of casual observation, you can tell that this wife just doesn't have a lot of respect for her husband. Even if she loves him, she doesn't trust him. And we aren't just talking about big trust issues. It flows over into how they spend money, where they go on vacation, and how they discipline the kids. He takes orders from her.

This can happen even if you are married to a strong man. Your husband might be admired and successful outside your home, but you have staked your claim as the one in charge at home. When your husband comes home, he obediently lays down his "man card." He may have a team of assistants and sales reps that jump at his every command at the office, but at home, he's the one taking the orders. "Clean up after yourself? I'm not your personal maid."

When a woman becomes dominant, it isn't a conscious decision. Usually, she's just reacting to passivity or weakness in her husband. Sometimes it's how she has learned to cope with the chaos of her childhood. She only feels safe if she's in charge. Maybe that's the only way she has ever seen marriage done. Her dad was weak and the mom was the boss.

Sarcastic Samantha

Humor is a gift from God. I'm blessed to be married to a very funny husband who makes me laugh almost every day. Sarcastic or biting humor is a different animal. I've met women who jokingly say, "Sarcasm is my spiritual gift." Probably not.

Instead of building her husband's confidence, a wife can easily use sarcastic or critical words to destroy her husband's capacity to lead. What wife hasn't flippantly said things that undermine a man's masculinity?

"Nice work, Einstein! A three-year-old could have figured that out."

"Yes, that's right. Who's bringing in more money?"

"Are you always so dull, or is today a special occasion?"

"I don't have the energy to like you today."

One person described sarcasm as punching you in the face with words. Even though you may just be joking, sarcasm usually is a backhanded way of expressing frustration and anger. But rather than address the issue, it cuts down your husband.

> **Even though you may just be joking, sarcasm usually is a backhanded way of expressing frustration and anger.**

Controlling Courtney

Have you ever walked into a house that looked absolutely perfect? Not a spot on the floor, nothing out of place, and even the dog sitting obediently in his crate? Unless the house is for sale, chances are someone living there is a bit of a control freak. Life is messy. Socks get lost, couches get stained, dust settles wherever it wants, and garbage smells like garbage. It takes constant effort to fight the messiness of a home.

The same can be said for marriage. A union between two people is messy. Not every conflict can be solved. Sometimes you're cranky or hungry or tired or depressed. Communication doesn't always bridge the gap between you.

Just like dealing with the mess of a home, some women approach the mess of marriage with control. Messes = anxiety. Your goal is to get rid of the anxiety by solving problems now and your way. Even better, you short-circuit the problem by controlling all the variables that might create tension, micromanaging to make sure things are done right.

No, the kids can't stay at your parents' house because they might feed them the wrong thing. No, the Rosses can't come over for dinner because you feel uncomfortable around the husband. We're not going on vacation in Mexico because my friend told me she got sick when she went. Don't pour the grape juice that way. It might spill on the carpet. If the dishes are to get cleaned, they have to be loaded in the dishwasher *this way*!

If this sounds familiar, you are likely controlling your way out of intimacy.

Rachel the Rescuer

Codependency is a pop psychology term that has been well-known since the recovery movement in the 1980s. Essentially, it means that you need someone to need you. Although you may not be crazy about someone's behavior, their weakness makes you feel validated and even irreplaceable. Without realizing it, some women reinforce their husband's immaturity and weaknesses because this has become the "glue" that keeps them together.

A rescuer may have been drawn to a spouse who needs a lot of help. This establishes a sense of security because your husband couldn't function without you. He needs you to be strong, and you need him to be weak.

There are situations in marriage when one person genuinely needs more help than the other—mental or physical illness or going through a season of grief or intense pressure. In family psychology, we refer to this as the sick role. Everyone needs to be in the sick role sometimes. A rescuer may place her husband in the sick role even when he doesn't need to be there. Because of her own need to be the strong one in the relationship, the rescuer won't invite her husband to grow into his strength. You are helping your ADHD husband by scheduling his doctor's appointment, but you are rescuing him when you become responsible for managing his calendar. Even if a husband has genuine limitations, he also has abilities and assets that he can contribute to his wife and to their relationship.

Juli the Jedi

The *Merriam-Webster* dictionary defines the word *manipulate* as "to change by artful or unfair means as to serve one's purpose." When I manipulate, I don't want to openly challenge Mike, but I also don't trust him. And so, rather than go through the hard work of conflict, I use subtle strategies to get him to do what I want. I use my power to suppress rather than to empower him.

I now have a built-in accountability as a wife because my husband has read this book and heard me teach these principles countless times. He's never gone so far as to point me to a page number or quote me when I use my power to take over, but he's definitely more aware of my strategies. One evening, we were hashing out some disagreement. In the middle of my sentence, Mike put up a finger and said, "Wait a minute. Before you say another word, I need to do something." He then slowly raised his hands in front of his face, just like an electric car window going up. "My manipulator shield is now activated. Go ahead and finish what you were saying." Another time he told me, "Don't try those Jedi mind tricks on me!"

My Jedi mind tricks are when I cross the line from influencing Mike to stacking the deck against him. For example, earlier in our marriage I would sometimes ask my dad to talk to Mike about something we disagreed about. I wouldn't tell Mike about this, but I'd give my dad talking points on what I thought would help Mike see things my way. Magically, he would then agree with me because Mike really respected my dad. While it's great that my dad could be a mentor for Mike, I manipulated situations by using the back door rather than just letting their relationship unfold.

Wives manipulate when we don't want to seem overbearing or bossy but we still want to be in control by pulling strings behind the scenes to get our way. For example, Karen knows Josh doesn't want a new suit, but she thinks he looks dumpy in his old one. So, Karen buys a suit without Josh knowing. When he protests, she says, "Oh, I'm sorry. This was a final sale and I can't take it back! I really thought you'd like it."

> Wives manipulate when we don't want to seem overbearing or bossy but we still want to be in control by pulling strings behind the scenes to get our way.

We can also manipulate by our appropriately timed tears or leveraging guilt. These strategies compromise our husbands' right to state their own opinion while we subtly use our power to get what we want.

Brittany the Back-Seat Driver

While we lived in Colorado, we often took advantage of the beautiful mountains. I'm the only skier in the family. Mike and the boys all prefer snowboarding. One day on the slopes, we all went up the lifts together and Mike told me, "You pick the first run." So, I picked a blue run that had some moguls. When we got to the bottom of the run, Mike said, "Why did you pick that one? The moguls were terrible for snowboarding!" I let Mike pick the runs the rest of the day. This experience gave me empathy for why husbands choose not to step up.

Who wants to make a decision knowing that it will come back to haunt him if things go wrong? Life is filled with tough decisions and judgment calls. Sometimes the right choice is impossible to discern, but hindsight is 20/20.

Even worse than being criticized for a decision is when you hear the words "I told you so." If a husband knows that his wife will let him have it if his decision is wrong, he will naturally approach leadership with more fear. "I'll let her decide and face the chance of being wrong." Or he might choose to do what his wife wants so that she can never blame him for making the wrong decision.

There are times in a marriage when saying or even implying "I told you so" seems absolutely necessary. You may feel vindicated when your instincts turn out to be right. Sometimes even a gloating glance is enough to communicate, "If only you would have listened to me!"

Whenever those four words (*I told you so!*) scream to be spoken, they are in reality totally unnecessary. A husband knows when his wife was right. To put it under his nose can result in only two things: He will become passive or more desperate to prove that he is in charge. Neither outcome builds your marriage.

When you were right but resist the temptation to tell him so, your encouragement will go a long way in building your

When you were right but resist the temptation to tell him so, your encouragement will go a long way in building your husband's trust in you.

husband's trust in you. Instead of reminding him that you were right, show grace. He will feel less threatened and more willing to value your input in the future. By refusing to remind him of his failure, you might give up an immediate opportunity to gain the upper hand, but you move closer to becoming a truly influential wife.

Okay, So How Do I Resign from My Position as the Boss?

The tactics I've described in this chapter may work in managing the chaos of your marriage, but they also undermine the chance for intimacy. Are you ready to consider a different approach? Anna was.

As a registered nurse, Anna is the sole wage earner in her marriage. Her husband, Caleb, has been working toward a counseling degree for the past few years but spends much of his "study time" playing on the computer, working out, and relaxing with friends. When Anna gets home from ten-hour shifts, she inevitably finds dirty laundry scattered on the floor and dishes in the sink. Sometimes, she fumes silently. Other days, she explodes in anger. When they argue, Caleb points to the fact that Anna has an unreasonable expectation of tidiness. He explains how stressed he feels by school and how unnatural it is for him to think of housework: "My mom always took care of that stuff."

From this description, Caleb seems like a lazy, immature husband who needs to grow up. But here's the kicker. A counselor could have explained Caleb's frustration with Anna just as effectively. Caleb could justifiably share stories of Anna encouraging (maybe even pushing him) to get a master's degree. He would remind Anna that she's the one who wanted to work full-time so he could go to school. This was all her idea, not his. Caleb might tell the story of what happened last week when he cooked dinner and cleaned the apartment. As soon as Anna walked through the door, she complained about the smell of burnt toast and ended up redoing most of the work Caleb had done.

Here's the point: Anna and Caleb have created a dance that prevents both of them from growing in maturity and intimacy. If Anna can lovingly and wisely change her contribution to their dance, this couple has a greater chance of thriving together.

If I were having coffee with a friend like Anna who was asking me how to change this dance, here are five practical suggestions I would give.

Humble Yourself

About three years into my marriage, God began to show me something really ugly—my pride. I genuinely believed that I knew how to do pretty much everything better than my husband did. Even when I yielded to his opinions and ideas, I did so almost with a patronizing attitude, *"Although I know I'm right, I'll encourage your leadership."* Do you know what I realized? I'm not always right. In fact, I'm wrong a lot. And many times, the issues Mike and I disagree on are not even a matter of right or wrong. Our approaches are just different. It has taken me a long, long time to let God chip away my pride. He's still working on me. Not long ago, I had this thought, *I think I'm more spiritually mature than my husband.* The Lord quickly revealed to me that the very fact that I had that thought revealed my immaturity!

Spiritual maturity means growing in grace, love, gratitude, humility, patience, and self-control. Genuine growth means that my husband looks better to me every day, not worse, because God is giving me the eyes to see Mike through His love.

In Philippians 2, Paul tells Christians, "If you have any

encouragement from being united with Christ, if any comfort from his love, if any common sharing in the Spirit, if any tenderness and compassion, then make my joy complete by being like-minded, having the same love, being one in spirit and of one mind. Do nothing out of selfish ambition or vain conceit. Rather, in humility value others above yourselves, not looking to your own interests but each of you to the interests of the others" (Phil. 2:1–4).

Genuine growth means that my husband looks better to me every day, not worse, because God is giving me the eyes to see Mike through His love.

What if you applied this lens of humility to how you see your husband? What would happen if you truly accepted him and stopped trying to change him? As I asked the Lord to teach me to do this, I began seeing strengths in my husband that my pride had kept me from appreciating.

Start with What You Have

As personality tests like the Enneagram, StrengthsFinder 2.0, and Myers-Briggs point out, every strength has a corresponding weakness. Your husband's personality is like two sides of a coin. This means the weaknesses that drive you crazy also have corresponding strengths. For instance,

- A charming, outgoing husband is the life of the party but may be demanding or manipulative in relationships.

- A reliable, detailed husband brings stability but may be emotionally dull.

- A passionate man who wants to change the world may make you proud, but he may also never sit still enough for you to share life with him.

Here's the point. Your husband has inborn strengths that probably are part of the reason you married him, but those strengths also come with weaknesses. If you want to change the dynamics of your marriage, you have to build on the strengths he has rather than trying to make him into a different man.

Let's go back to Caleb. While this young husband has given Anna some reason to complain, he's also a genuinely caring guy. He may not wash the dishes in the sink, but he spent several hours last week helping an elderly neighbor with her new computer. He has great gifts of mercy and compassion and would be the first to sacrifice for a friend in need. If Anna would like to see her husband mature, her best bet is to build on what he naturally does well. She did this by encouraging him to get his counseling degree. This doesn't feel like it's paying off right now, but someday, it will.

Your husband is a leader, but he may not be wired to lead the way you want him to. You have to look for the inborn paths of leadership that God has given him and trust him to lead within his personality.

Invite His Strength by Revealing Your Weakness

When our three boys were very little, I was overwhelmed and exhausted much of the time. There were days when I wanted to meet my husband at the door with a demand, "Why are you late? I've taken care of them all day. It's your turn. I need a break!" If I had that tone, Mike would have shut down or spent ten minutes telling me how much more stressful his day was than mine. I have a very caring husband who is eager to help me, but he will never respond well to being told what to do. As a young, independent woman, I had to learn to invite Mike's help by showing him my weakness. This was not easy for me. I liked to convince myself and everyone else around that I could handle *anything*. This strategy left me with handling *everything* and resenting it. I learned to say, "I'm overwhelmed. I need you. Can you please help me?"

I used to think that being a great wife meant never showing him my weaknesses. Actually, the opposite is true. If I'm never weak, there's no need for a hero. There is no room for your husband's strength if you refuse to acknowledge your limitations.

Instead of feeling angry and disappointed in Caleb, Anna may have gotten much further by showing him her legitimate weakness and appealing to his sensitivity. "Caleb, I understand that housework isn't your thing and I know that school is stressful. But I'm about to fall apart. I'm so tired when I get home at the end of a shift. I really need you. Can we figure out a way to tackle this as a team?"

> If I'm never weak, there's no need for a hero. There is no room for your husband's strength if you refuse to acknowledge your limitations.

Stop Rescuing Him

At the root of many immature husbands is silence: his refusal to assume responsibility, to step into leadership, and to become the servant leader he was created to emulate. Within the silence is a void that begs to be filled. You may not fill it with words, but you take over when your husband hesitates. He forgot to pay the electric bill, so you take care of it. He doesn't make enough money, so you increase your hours at work to fill in the shortfall. The kids are screaming while he scrolls through videos on his phone, so you jump in and parent. Before you know it, you have assumed the vast majority of responsibilities.

Think of it like a conversation. If one person does all the talking, the other person never has to say anything. Whenever there is silence, don't fill it. Give him room to feel the tension of that *silence*. This might mean short-term inconvenience and stress, but it is a small price if it can help you establish a healthier dance.

You may not like this suggestion, but it's an important part of helping your husband grow. Resist the urge to step in when he doesn't step up. If something is clearly his responsibility, don't nag. Don't complain. Don't do anything. If the power gets shut off, so be it. If the lawn hasn't been mowed all summer, let it go. Have honest, constructive conversations about the issue (maybe with a counselor), but don't take up the slack. This may be extremely difficult for you because you're afraid of what might happen if... (you fill in the blank). There may be some situations where you have to step in because of safety, but in most cases, the consequences of stepping back are worth the reward of watching your husband learn to step forward.

Let Him Grow into Manhood, Not Womanhood

While we would never say it so openly, we often define maturity by what we value *as women*, things like sensitivity, communication, spiritual devotion, and appropriately responding to every imaginable interpersonal situation.

Mature masculinity looks different from mature femininity. Even how a man may display sensitivity, communication, and spiritual devotion can look different than it does in your life. Sometimes we give our guys grief for being men. Why is reading to your child more valuable than roughhousing? And why is it less mature to play video games than to spend three hours on Instagram? And even within the culture of manhood, healthy masculinity can look very different from one guy to another. Be careful not to define maturity by a narrow set of standards.

While you can encourage your husband to be a hero, you can't teach him how to be a man. Men have to be validated by other men. They need to be taught things they may have never learned from their father. Caleb doesn't need Anna to give him a lesson on cleaning the house and the wonders of the Instant Pot. He needs a seasoned, wise man to show him how to manage his time and challenge him to love his wife well.

Male friends and mentors are an invaluable piece of maturity. Many guys won't respond well to the suggestion to get a mentor. You might start by asking questions like "Who do you admire (at work, church, in your family?)" You can also encourage mentoring by spending time with older couples who can pass on wisdom. Whatever the cost, invest in relationships that help you both grow. If your husband interacts with mature, godly men while hunting deer, clear the calendar during hunting season!

My friend, I know that you are frustrated by your husband's lack of maturity and willingness to take responsibility. I understand that you really believe you do things better than your husband does them. You fear that if you don't step in, things will fall apart. But it is key for you to understand that you are the one person who ultimately can invite your husband into the challenges of authentic relationship and adult life. Even more than the fear of dropping the ball, your husband fears failing you.

As his wife, you have the delicate role of protecting your husband's vulnerabilities while also calling forth his strengths. It sounds complicated, but it is accomplished day by day, moment by moment by how you choose to think about him, pray for him, and respond to him. The wonderful news is that you aren't the first woman to walk through the challenges of how to bring out the man in your husband. I've seen it done by wise women, and I'm learning the art of doing so in my own marriage. I've learned when to step back, when to encourage, and when to confront.

When I've shared this perspective before, some women have responded with anger. "Why is it my fault that my husband won't grow up?" and "Stop blaming females for men's sin!" Let me be very clear. Some men come into marriage with insecurity, addictions, or a hard heart that is unwilling to change. God doesn't hold us responsible for our husbands' weaknesses or sin. However, we are responsible for how we respond to our circumstances. If God has truly given you more maturity, wisdom, and strength than your husband, this means that you have much more power in your relationship than he does. How are you using that power?

Remember, You Are Not Without a Net

Every woman will, at some point, experience the fear of trusting a husband who is capable of making drastic mistakes. No one can promise you that your husband won't lose his job, squander your savings, or cheat on you. As we discussed in the last chapter, there are times when you need to be very assertive in setting boundaries and protecting both yourself and your husband from his weaknesses. But most often, women take over because we don't know how to trust. Trusting is incredibly difficult, especially when you intimately know your husband's weakness and immaturity.

Here's what you need to remember. Investing in your husband is not ultimately about trusting him but trusting God. You may feel like you are walking a tightrope, but you have a safety net.

I remember one particularly miserable time in my marriage. Mike and I had a major fight about a serious issue. I was hurt and angry. As he drove off, I yelled something like "Sure. Leave! Don't bother coming back!" I ran into the house where my three small boys were waiting. I remember closing myself in the pantry and sobbing. I felt hopeless. If you had given me the book *Finding the Hero in Your Husband,* I might have thrown it at you. My comfort in moments like this one did not come from imagining how wonderful our marriage could be, but from running to the God who sees me, who loves me, and who has promised to be with me.

The bigger battle of your marriage is not learning to trust your husband but choosing to trust your Lord. Bible teacher Beth Moore has shared a mental exercise she goes through with the Lord whenever she is afraid. She imagines her worst fears, like *what if my husband has an affair or falls in love with another woman?* Then what? She describes how she would cry out to God in pain. She would beg Him to redeem the pain to bear eternal fruit, as He has promised to do so many times in Scripture. Even if the worst happens, "By His grace, I'm going to get back up....Let's get back to living."[ii]

Friend, there is nothing and no one who can separate you from your purpose and the love of God for you. This is not to belittle your fears or pain; they are real! But so is your God, Redeemer, and Savior. Do you know Him? Do you trust Him enough to stop protecting yourself? Will you lean on Him to give you the courage to be the wise wife who builds?

Endnotes

i   https://www.goodreads.com/quotes/80515-the-only-thing-worse-than-a
    -man-you-can-t-control.

ii https://www.youtube.com/watch?v=Og_4ZfWYcH4.

♥

Chapter 7

your last fight

Tyler and Jackie couldn't wait for some time away. Life had been stressful juggling two full-time jobs and three children. Finally, they would have some space to sleep, laugh, talk, and enjoy sex without a child knocking on the door. Tyler's parents watched the kids while they enjoyed a six-night romantic getaway for their tenth anniversary.

Within the first twenty-four hours of their vacation, Tyler and Jackie were no longer speaking. If not for the embarrassment of coming home early and expensive flight changes, they may have just called the vacation off. Staying in a hotel room for a week with a king-size bed suddenly felt like torture. What had gone wrong?

It began with little things. Their flight was delayed, meaning they arrived at their hotel close to midnight. They were both tired and crabby. Tyler turned on the TV while Jackie tried to sleep. The next morning, Jackie was ready for some uninterrupted sex, but Tyler wanted to work out and eat breakfast first. By lunchtime, the tension in their mismatched expectations surfaced with forced conversation. They tried to brush it off, relaxing by the pool with piña coladas. Then

Jackie saw Tyler admiring a beautiful woman in a string bikini. When she commented about it, Tyler responded, "What? I just looked. It's not like I'm flirting with her or anything. How could a guy not notice *that*?" Then Jackie let him have it. All her frustration from the past year flooded out on him. His inappropriate sense of humor. His insensitivity. His unwillingness to listen or make her feel special.

"Babe," Tyler said. "What are you talking about? I've been saving for six months to take you on this trip. And now you want to fight? Nice timing! I'd have been better off going camping with the guys."

Nothing ruins the romance of marriage like an unexpected fight. Within the course of a few minutes, you can go from contentment to combat. One simple word or action can unlock the anger and fear you've been storing up for months.

What if I told you that you and your husband can be married and never fight again? Would you believe me? Okay. That might be a bit of an optimistic promise, but it's a vision I believe you can work toward. As I write this, my husband and I haven't had a fight for almost a full year. (Although now that I've written this, we are destined for one!) And when we do fight, we know how to recover without deeply wounding each other and our marriage.

In this chapter, I want to share with you some truths that Mike and I are learning to apply that have drastically changed how we address conflict.

A Conflict Is Not the Same Thing as a Fight

What is the difference between fighting and conflict? Isn't *conflict* just a nicer way of saying "fight"? Actually, no. A conflict in your marriage is any difference between you and your husband.

It can be something as simple as he likes Starbucks and you like Dunkin' Donuts coffee. Or he likes the bedroom freezing cold and you don't. A conflict is not a mini-fight. Conflicts can be very significant. You want to quit your job and he depends on your income. You love Jesus, but he doesn't believe God exists. Your husband thinks it's okay to look at a woman in a bikini and you don't! These are conflicts but not yet fights.

Any conflict, big or little, becomes a fight when a few things happen:

One of you gets triggered. A trigger is something that happens in the here and now that brings up suppressed feelings and experiences. It's like the small noise that wakes up a sleeping dog. A trigger reminds you, even subconsciously or biologically, of significant wounds and fears.

Let's go back to Tyler and Jackie. There had been stress and unaddressed tension building for many months. The busyness of life allowed them to maintain a workable relationship with little intimacy. Time alone without the noise and distractions brought it all to the surface. While the little things felt irritating, Jackie was triggered by Tyler's admiration of the bikini lady. When Tyler's gaze lingered, Jackie was reminded of many other times she doubted her husband's affection. Underneath that fear was the memory of her father walking out on her mother because he fell in love with another woman. And so, Jackie is not just addressing the conflict in the here and now but also reacting to all that this scenario represents for her. Jackie's reaction then triggered Tyler. He wanted to surprise Jackie with this special vacation, planning for his parents to watch the kids. He'd spent hours putting together the details and looked forward to a stress-free, fun time with his wife. Now, less than one day into their special time together, she was yelling at him, scolding him, shaming him. "You blew it again, Bonehead."

When one of you gets triggered, you no longer see the conflict as something to address. Instead, you react to a tsunami of emotions a conflict may represent. Going to McDonalds instead of Subway isn't a big issue, but what if that choice represents all the times your voice wasn't heard or your opinion valued? (Notice that our triggers often tie into our deepest needs as husbands and wives.)

Safety becomes more important than intimacy. When we get triggered, we feel threatened. Dr. John Gottman is known as one of the leading marriage experts in the world. He has been able to predict near the beginning of a relationship which couples will stay together and who will divorce with astounding accuracy of over 90 percent.[i] How does he do it? Through his "love lab." Dr. Gottman hooked up men and women to a number of physiological measures of stress levels and then introduced conflict into the conversation and recorded what happened.

Dr. Gottman found that for toxic couples, conflict led to a severe feeling of threat and little empathy between partners. Their disagreements were characterized by what Gottman called the four horsemen of the apocalypse: criticism, defensiveness, contempt, and stonewalling.[ii] Marital stability is not based on whether or not a couple has conflict, but how they manage conflict.

> **Marital stability is not based on whether or not a couple has conflict, but how they manage conflict.**

When your marriage is in a bad place, conflict can make you feel like your very survival is at stake. You and your husband instinctively kick into fight or flight. At the moment, you don't care about your marriage. You care about protecting your heart.

When your bo*dy* is filled with cortisol and adrenaline (stress hormones), your critical thinking skills, long-term reasoning, and empathy take a back seat. You literally react from a different part of your brain. You will make your best relational decisions when you're thinking with your cerebral cortex. This area of the brain allows you to think rationally and to experience empathy for other people. When you feel threatened, you react with other parts of the brain, including the amygdala and the prefrontal cortex. These areas of the brain are important for survival, but they do a lousy job of building intimacy.

You protect with "backup styles." Each one of us has learned (usually from childhood) a unique style of reacting to this type of relational stress. You don't even have to think about it. It just happens. While everyone's "fighting clothes" are a little bit different, there are common themes in how we fight or take flight. Here are a few of them. As you read through them, realize that they could represent either you or your husband. Both of you have a backup style that comes out when you feel threatened.

- ❤ **The Incredible Hulk.** The Hulk isn't aware of feeling sad or scared. All those emotions are covered with anger, which feels much less vulnerable than crying or backing away. Anger allows a person to temporarily feel in control of the situation. Ironically, an angry person isn't in control of herself. She lashes out with hurtful words and threats without thinking through the consequences or considering the feelings of the other person.

- ❤ **Invisibility Cloak.** Now you see her, now you don't! When threatened by conflict, the strategy is to get far away from the anxiety of the situation. She has friends, family, hobbies, and fantasies to run to in conflict because she absolutely hates tension. When things heat up, it's time to peace out.

❦ **The Intimidator.** She follows her spouse around the house, spewing an endless stream of words, demanding that he talk this through right now, or sends dozens of texts shouting in all caps, followed by exclamation points and less-than-friendly emojis. These are intimidation strategies. The intimidator congratulates herself as the one who wants to work on the problem rather than run away from it. In reality, she doesn't want to resolve the conflict but stay in control by overpowering her spouse.

❦ **The Pacifier.** "What did I do? Just let me know how I can make you feel better!" Blessed are the peacemakers. Didn't Jesus say this? So why would it be wrong to try to smooth over conflict? The pacifier doesn't want to resolve conflict; she wants to avoid it by immediately assuming all responsibility for what went wrong or giving in to her husband's perspective. Conflict is an essential element of intimacy. It requires give-and-take, listening and talking for both parties. When a pacifier shortcuts this process, she enables selfishness. For the sake of peace in the moment, she compromises any opportunity to forge unity in marriage.

❦ **The Lawyer.** The lawyer genuinely believes that fighting is resolved by the person with the better argument. While she won't rage or insult, she will eloquently and doggedly make the case with facts, history, and conviction that he's guilty and she's innocent. Her goal is to prove that she is right. The lawyer can be absolutely dumbfounded when the jury is not impressed. Her brilliant argument does nothing to convince her husband, who just stands there unmoved in his own "fighting clothes."

All these styles are based on a fundamentally flawed approach to conflict. The goal of conflict is not to win or gain the upper hand. It's not even to compromise or to solve the problem. *The goal of conflict is ultimately to understand each other more completely.* All the strategies previously described are ways that we've learned to cope with a threatening relational moment, but they ultimately build walls rather than move us toward unity.

You can spend years building intimacy and then tear down what you've built in ten minutes of fighting. When conflict slides into fighting, we say things without thinking through the consequences. We unload stored up frustrations, anger, and criticism. We put up walls that prevent us from seeing and hearing our husbands' heart or them from seeing ours.

This is why it's absolutely essential to learn the difference between conflict and fighting. *You will always have conflict in your marriage, but fighting is optional.*

You will always have conflict in your marriage, but fighting is optional.

A Different Approach to Conflict

You and your husband will always have problems to address, some of them small and some of them very consequential. These conflicts may actually facilitate deeper intimacy in your marriage if you learn to handle them wisely. But first, it's critical that you both learn to catch yourself from falling into fighting. Here are some fundamental differences between healthy conflict and fighting:

Fighting Versus Healthy Conflict

FIGHTING	HEALTHY CONFLICT
Impulsive—driven by emotions	Intentional—guided by concern
Motivated by fear, anger, pride	Motivated by desire for deeper intimacy
Me against you	Us against a problem
Goal: to prove that I'm right or maintain control	Goal: to understand each other and make wise decisions
Dress ourselves in fighting clothes	Ask God to dress me
Ends when damage has been done or one person has "won"	Ends when you both have a deeper understanding of the other and the issue

To walk this out, let's look at an example of how a couple can choose between fighting and healthy conflict.

Jose recently took a new job as the family pastor at a local church. This is his first ministry role after years of working in the corporate world. His wife, Maria, is totally supportive of this career change. Together, they chose to make the sacrifices of a pay cut for Jose to follow God's call into ministry.

When Valentine's Day came around, Maria had the normal expectations of a romantic evening with her husband. She asked Jose what the plans were, and Jose texted, "I forgot to tell you, but we have a church event that night."

On the surface, here is the conflict. Maria wanted to go out together. Jose planned a church event.

A Fight Will Be Impulsive While Healthy Conflict Is Intentional

When Maria reads Jose's text informing her of his unromantic Valentine's Day plans, she feels a rush of hurt and anger. If Maria responds to her feelings in the moment, this probably isn't going to go well. One of the fruits of the Spirit is self-control. It takes a lot of self-control to not give in to your immediate feelings of fear or anger when there is conflict. Please note, this does not mean that you avoid or forget about the conflict. It means that you address it intentionally when it's the right time and you have the right heart.

Instead of texting Jose back to say how hurt she is, she might text something like "got it" and then plan to bring the conflict up with him when he gets home from work.

> One of the biggest mistakes couples make in conflict is insisting that they have to address the issue right now.

One of the biggest mistakes couples make in conflict is insisting that they have to address the issue right now. I've talked to couples who try to talk through a conflict in the middle of the night or when they are hungry, stressed, or surrounded by friends. Some couples think they have to address conflict right now because of the verse, "Don't let the sun go down on your anger."[iii] In this verse, Paul is talking about not going to bed with bitterness and anger in your heart. This is an issue of keeping short accounts between you and God, not between you and your husband. There are many times you will need to confess and deal with your anger before God, way before you are ready to have the right kind of conflict with your husband.

A Fight Is Motivated by Fear, Anger, or Pride; A Conflict Is Motivated by a Desire for Deeper Intimacy

This is not the first time Jose has forgotten to tell Maria that he would miss an important event. They never celebrated Christmas last year because the church needed him. In the last six months, he'd missed birthdays, their son's basketball games, and important family gatherings. Maria has had enough. She wants to unload on her husband all the feelings of rejection and hurt she's buried since he took his new job. Reacting to strong feelings will lead to a fight. In truth, Jose has his own feelings of fear, anger, or pride that will come out if they start fighting. He feels the pressure to succeed in his new role and resents the fact that doing well at work means having to face Maria's anger and disappointment over and over again.

If Maria and Jose are to engage in healthy conflict, they need to realize that this new job situation has created a chasm between them. They are growing apart as they have demands and feelings that the other person doesn't understand. For their marriage to be intimate, they have to reconnect and get on the same page.

Based on Dr. Gottman's research, one of the most critical skills you can develop as a married couple is what he calls a *repair*. This is the ability to recognize when you are sliding into a fight and to do something that stops that dangerous momentum. Gottman describes it as "any statement or action—silly or otherwise—that prevents negativity from escalating out of control."[iv]

This is really hard to do, but you can get better at it with preparation and practice. A repair might be just saying, "I'm going down a bad road right now. I just need some time." Or even some light-hearted (*not* sarcastic) humor can help change the environment. My husband has gotten really good at stepping in when his anger starts to take over. He will often say, "I don't want to fight with you. I'm on your team." Sometimes we have the self-control to pray together instead of fight, recognizing that the enemy wants to divide us. These repairs don't mean we ignore the conflict. The repair gives us perspective on how to approach the conflict at a healthier time with the right motives.

Conflict Is Us Against a Problem While Fighting Is Me Against You

A fight will always be about me versus you. As much as Maria may support Jose's decision to go into ministry, she doesn't support how he is managing his time in this new role. His choices are hurting her and their family, and Jose is beginning to resent his wife. She may not say anything, but he can tell that she's angry when he comes home late. What is he supposed to do? Family ministry happens when people aren't working. That means evenings and weekends. She's putting him in a situation where he either fails at work or fails at home.

A different way of approaching this conflict is for Jose and Maria to view this situation as a problem they need to solve as a team. They decided together to make this job change and it impacts both of them. Now it's time for them to find ways to be a family, to celebrate holidays, and to work on intimacy within the demands of ministry life. To do this, they need to take turns understanding and validating each other's feelings.

In Fighting, the Goal Is to Prove That I'm Right or to Maintain the Upper Hand; in Healthy Conflict, the Goal Is to Understand Each Other and to Make Wise Decisions

When a couple like Jose and Maria have drifted apart because of busyness, stress, or disappointment, they lose touch with each other's hearts. Their communication can become transactional (who's picking up Sam from basketball?) and caustic (You *know* I can't do it. I have a staff meeting!). The Valentine's Day conflict presents either an opportunity to unload in self-protection mode or to say, "We have a problem. We are drifting apart. I want to get back on the same team and reconnect with your heart."

Instead of Wearing "Fighting Clothes," Healthy Conflict Means We Let God Dress Us

Earlier in the chapter, I described some of the ways we get dressed for a fight. These are unconscious strategies we use to stay safe when we feel emotionally threatened.

Maria and Jose have their set ways of approaching conflict. She gets angry and he avoids, becoming resentful. God asks this couple to dress differently for conflict. Colossians 3 offers a very practical passage on how to "dress" for conflict.

> But now you must put them all away: anger, wrath, malice, slander, and obscene talk from your mouth. Do not lie to one another, seeing that you have put off the old self with its practices and have put on the new self, which is being renewed in knowledge after the image of its creator.

> Put on then, as God's chosen ones, holy and beloved, compassionate hearts, kindness, humility, meekness, and patience, bearing with one another and, if one has a complaint against another, forgiving each other; as the Lord has forgiven you, so you also must forgive. And above all these put on love, which binds everything together in perfect harmony. And let the peace of Christ rule in your hearts, to which indeed you were called in one body. And be thankful. Let the word of Christ dwell in you richly, teaching and admonishing one another in all wisdom,

singing psalms and hymns and spiritual songs, with thankfulness in your hearts to God. And whatever you do, in word or deed, do everything in the name of the Lord Jesus, giving thanks to God the Father through Him. (Col. 3:8–17 NIV)

This passage tells us what to take off when we are preparing for conflict: anger, wrath, malice (the desire to hurt my husband), slander (damaging someone's reputation), foul language, and dishonesty.

Then, it tells us what to put on: compassion, kindness, humility, meekness, patience, forgiveness, and love. We are able to put on these clothes by remembering what God has done for us, being thankful for His work in our lives, and being rooted in His Word.

Let me ask you, have you ever approached a conflict with your husband by preparing like this? Or do you rush into difficult conversations determined to come out on top? You can win every argument with your husband and still lose your marriage.

You can win every argument with your husband and still lose your marriage.

Fighting Ends When Damage Has Been Done or Someone Wins; Healthy Conflict Ends When You Have a Deeper Understanding of Each Other

Dr. John Gottman made an astonishing statement based on his research on marriage and conflict: *"about two-thirds of all conflicts between partners are unsolvable."*[v] Yes, you read that right. Most of the things you and your husband argue about don't have a compromise or a solution. If you are a saver and your husband is a spender, that's never going to change. You are destined to have conflict over money issues for your entire marriage. If your love language is quality time together and your husband is driven to prove his worth through work, you will be fighting for years about how he spends his time.

The good news is that the goal of healthy conflict is *not to solve your irreconcilable differences* but to understand them and learn to navigate them. Financial planner Larry Burkett once said, "If two people just alike get married, one of you is unnecessary."[vi] The unresolvable differences between you and your husband do not have to be a barrier to intimacy, they can actually be the road map. Differences force us to love in a manner that costs us something.

> The good news is that the goal of healthy conflict is *not to solve your irreconcilable differences* but to understand them and learn to navigate them.

The nature of true love is that it requires sacrifice. If you and your husband could compromise on every issue, you would never learn to love the way God loves you. Marriage is not just a metaphor for God's love; it is also the vehicle that invites us to imitate it.

Intimacy between Maria and Jose will at best get stuck if they ignore the conflict they are currently experiencing in their marriage. If they slide into fighting, they will chip away at the safety of their relationship. But if they can view this conflict as an invitation to learn to love, then the conflict itself can stretch both of them to mature. This is a much greater and more significant goal than figuring out what to do on Valentine's Day.

Learning a New Way

There is no question that we each bring a lot of baggage into marriage. In general, we fight the way we saw our parents fight. We have trigger points based on deep wounds that happened before marriage and ways that we've hurt each other in the past. A lot of learning to handle conflict well is identifying patterns and triggers that pull us into unhealthy conflict. I'm a big fan of marriage mentoring and counseling to help people get to these roots that often sabotage intimacy, but there are also some basic skills you and your husband can learn to approach conflict differently. Below are seven steps to healthy conflict. These steps might take fifteen minutes or they may take several days, depending on the conflict. They are steps that I use not only in my marriage, but also when I have conflict at work, with my kids, or in friendships.

STEP 1: Identify the Problem

A lot of times we identify superficial problems without realizing that the obvious issue is a symptom of something more significant.

Once a month, Rachel and Bryon have a date night. "Where do you want to go to dinner tonight?" Rachel says, "I don't care. You pick." So, Bryon makes reservations at a Thai restaurant. Rachel is in a bad mood while she picks at her curry chicken. When Bryon asks about it, she says, "You know I hate Thai food."

The obvious conflict is where they like to eat dinner on date nights. The deeper issue is that Rachel is upset that her husband didn't consider what she likes when he chose the reservation (hint: she doesn't feel valued). Bryon is confused because he asked her and she didn't have an opinion (hint: he feels set up for failure).

Identifying the real problem might take some time, prayer, and perspective. You might need to ask yourself, *Why did I feel so angry or irritated when that happened?* By pinpointing what's really going on in your heart, you won't waste time and energy fighting about things that only matter because of what they symbolize.

STEP 2: Prepare the Ground

Preparing the ground means making sure that the time is right to approach conflict well. You can prepare your own heart by going through a passage like Colossians 3, asking the Lord to give you the right perspective. Choosing the right time and place to address conflict is also important.

I remember one romantic getaway Mike and I had several years ago during the busy parenting years. We were having a great time sleeping, connecting, and doing fun things together. On our last day, we were casually walking around a beautiful lake and I brought up a very sensitive conflict. In my mind, this was the perfect time because we'd been able to rest and enjoy each other for a few days. My husband's angry reaction told me a different story.

Once Mike and I processed this, he said he felt like I blind-sided him. He was relaxed, having fun, and his guard was down. By bringing up the issue, he felt like I threw a grenade when he had no defenses. I was ready for the conversation, but I didn't give him the chance to prepare for it.

Mike helped me understand that if I'm going to bring up a difficult conflict, I need to let him know so he can prepare. So now, I will say something like "There's something that's on my heart that I need to share with you. When within the next few days would be a good time for us to talk?"

STEP 3: State the Problem

Remember, your husband is not the problem. The problem is the problem (even if he's contributed to it). There is a big difference between stating a problem these two ways:

"When we spend time with your parents, you always treat me like I don't matter. You take their side on everything, and you never stand up for us." (Notice words like you, always, everything, and never.)

Instead, you could address the same problem with these words:

"Last night when we were with your parents, I felt really hurt. The holidays came up and you went along with their suggestions. I felt hurt that you didn't give us the room to talk together about how we want to spend the holidays." (Notice this is one particular situation. Yes, it probably represents other times this has happened, but it's less threatening to be confronted with one situation than to be hit with a barrage of examples out of the gate. This wife is not attacking her husband's character. She is instead confronting him with how she feels.)

This is not the time to explain your perspective. That comes later! Now you are just putting the problem into play for your husband to share his thoughts and feelings.

STEP 4: Listen

Once you have stated the problem, it's time for you to listen. I'm sure you've entered a conflict completely convinced that your perspective is the right one, but after listening, the issue doesn't seem so cut and dry. You develop empathy for how your husband feels and views the same set of facts. This is such a critical step in conflict because it's where you give up your demand to get your own way, and you build the bridge to understanding your husband. By truly listening, you show you care about more than just winning an argument.

> **By truly listening, you show you care about more than just winning an argument.**

Unfortunately, a lot of people don't know how to listen. If you took a communications course in high school or college, you probably spent all your time learning to effectively communicate *your thoughts* and literally no time learning to hear anyone else's perspective. But communication requires both talking *and* listening. There is a right and a wrong way to listen:

- 💜 Listening is not zoning out until it's your turn to talk.

- 💜 Listening is not building your argument against what your husband is saying.

- 💜 Listening is the effort to learn about your husband. It involves straining with your heart to see his. You can use nonverbal encouragement for him to keep talking by leaning in, nodding your head, and making eye contact.

- 💜 Listening might include asking good follow-up questions like "Help me understand what you mean by that," "Have you ever felt that way before?" or "Why do you think you reacted that way?"

STEP 5: Validate

You can only validate someone if you have truly listened to him. Validation means that you've heard your husband and recognize his experience and how it differs from yours. This is key: you can validate your husband's thoughts and feelings without agreeing with them!

A validation might be "So, when I made that comment, you felt disrespected" or "You feel a lot of pressure to live up to your boss's expectations. That's a lot of stress to walk around with."

Validation also means taking responsibility for your part of the conflict. This does not mean capitulating to "You're right. I was wrong." Remember this is not about who wins an argument but about learning to love through differences. You might feel like your husband is 90 percent responsible for the problem. Then take responsibility for the 10 percent. Sometimes, this means acknowledging how you contributed without even realizing it. "I'm so sorry you felt that way. When I said that, I truly did not mean to hurt you."

In most situations, a person would rather be validated in conflict than win an argument.

In most situations, a person would rather be validated in conflict than win an argument. The conflict is not ultimately about being right or wrong but about being heard, seen, and understood. When you or your husband jump right to problem-solving or compromise, you will miss this critical step.

STEP 6: Share to Be Understood

Now is the time for you to help your husband understand how you feel. Again, the goal is not blaming or winning an argument. It's helping him see your heart.

One of the things Mike and I often have conflict around is his desire for things to be just right. This is a great quality—just today he reorganized our Tupperware cupboard! But it also means that he has a set way that he likes things to be done. When we spend a lot of time together, this grates on me. He tells me where to walk on a sidewalk, when is the best time of the day to eat carbs, and how I need to delegate more household chores to our sons. It's not that I disagree with his advice. I just don't like to feel controlled.

When Mike and I work through a conflict like this, he helps me to see that he doesn't want to control me. He thinks he's being helpful and protective. Many times, he is, but there is a fine line. When I feel like he's crossed that line, I need to do more than just say, "Back off!" I need to express how I like being independent. I don't want to be treated like a child who can't make decisions for myself, even if that's not what he's trying to do. I might give him specific examples that make me feel that way.

If I've validated Mike's perspective and communicated mine without blaming, my husband will many times validate how I feel.

STEP 7: Connecting Activity

While the work of addressing conflict involves listening to God and each other, this last step is the culmination of that work. It's not enough just to hear and understand. Now it's time to act.

A connecting activity can be as simple as a hug or as dramatic as renewing your vows, depending on the nature and length of a conflict. You might pray together or even have "makeup sex." The key is to do something to symbolize that you are on the same team, that you understand and care for each other.

Connecting might also be coming up with a solution as a team to address problems related to the conflict. For example, you and your husband might decide to read a parenting book together to get on the same page, meet with a counselor to work through an issue you can't agree on, or come up with a compromise that addresses both your needs.

The Uniqueness of a Christian Marriage

Throughout this chapter, I've shared some basic tips that can help every marriage more effectively address conflict. Dr. John Gottman's research is helpful and insightful, even though he isn't coming from a Christian perspective. While Christian and secular marriages have much in common, there is also some uniqueness that is worth noting, especially as it relates to conflict. Here are three differences to keep in mind as you navigate difficulties in your marriage:

You Have a Different Goal

When a typical couple seeks help for their marriage, their number one priority is to find happiness, or at least peace, in their relationship. Conflict is always the enemy because it spoils nirvana. The goal is to remove or resolve the conflict so you and your husband can continue in a relationship that demands as little as possible from you.

A Christian marriage has an entirely different goal. Yes, happiness in marriage is wonderful, but it is viewed as a byproduct of a more important objective: becoming more like Christ.

God could make your marriage easy. He could have brought you a soul mate with whom you would never disagree or be hurt by. Yet, He has put you, an imperfect person, with another imperfect person for the sake of learning about a perfect love. He will never waste pain that is yielded to Him!

You have a goal far greater than a happy marriage. God has called you to "be holy as He is holy." Marital conflict is a very effective "love lab" to accomplish His purposes in your life and heart.

Your Marriage Is a Spiritual Battle

When Jesus was asked about divorce, he responded, "From the beginning of creation, 'God made them male and female.' For this reason a man will leave his mother and father and be united to his wife, and the two will become one flesh.' So, they are no longer two

A godly marriage is a divine mystery, modeling for the participants and the watching world a miracle of love conquering selfishness.

but one flesh. Therefore, what God has joined together, let man not separate." There are few things that Satan hates more than a Christian marriage.

A godly marriage is a divine mystery, modeling for the participants and the watching world a miracle of love conquering selfishness. Satan doesn't care whether you are fighting over who should earn the money or what color to paint the living room as long as he can divide you.

There have been times in my marriage when it almost feels like Satan is whispering in my ear. "You deserve better than this. Mike is a jerk. You shouldn't put up with that." Mike has told me the same thing during seasons of conflict. All he can see are my weaknesses. It's taken years for us to learn that we must fight spiritual battles with spiritual weapons. As a psychologist, I know the tricks and techniques of my field, but psychology can't defeat Satan or my own sinful heart. We need to pray. We need to confess. We need to forgive. We need to ask God for help and claim the truths in His Word. "If God is for us, who can stand against us?"

You Have the Holy Spirit

One day while counseling with a friend, she joked, "Juli, I wish I could just take you home with me. You could give me the right words to say the next time my husband and I are in conflict." I reminded my friend that she *could* take home someone much wiser and more powerful than me. She has the presence of God through the Holy Spirit.

We get so familiar with a statement like this that we often fail to recognize the gravity of what it means. Imagine if you could take Jesus everywhere with you. What if in a moment of anger or depression, you could ask Him what to do? What if He could hold you and give you comfort?

This is what God has given as a deposit to everyone who trusts in Him! The Holy Spirit is described as the Comforter, the Counselor, your Advocate. He convicts you of sin, He seals your salvation, He is your Guide, your Intercessor, Revealer of Truth, your Teacher, and the very spirit of Jesus Christ.

Often, we don't experience the Holy Spirit this way. Why? Because He waits to be invited. The Bible says that we can "quench" the power of the Holy Spirit when we ignore Him. When I go down the path of selfishness, bitterness, and anger, I tell God that I don't want His help or comfort.

Jesus said that people would recognize His disciples by the way we love one another. Why? Because true love is only possible through the presence of the Holy Spirit. God calls you to be a faithful, loving wife, even in seasons of conflict. This is something you cannot do without His help.

The ultimate conflict in marriage is not my way versus my husband's way. It's my way versus yielding to the work of God in my life and marriage.

Endnotes

i https://www.gottman.com/about/research/faq/.

ii https://www.gottman.com/blog/the-four-horsemen-recognizing-criticism-contempt-defensiveness-and-stonewalling/.

iii Ephesians 4:26.

iv https://www.gottman.com/blog/r-is-for-repair/.

v https://www.gottman.com/blog/managing-conflict-solvable-vs-perpetual-problems/.

vi https://quotes.pub/larry-burkett-quotes.

Chapter 8

how did we get here?

A recent film about marriage begins in a heart-warming way. The husband and wife take turns reflecting on what they love most about each other. They give examples of thoughtfulness, adventure, and sensitivity as they reflect on their relationship. As a viewer, you are pulled into a beautiful love story of two quirky and caring people until you realize that the couple is meeting with a divorce counselor and seeking to dissolve their marriage. The rest of the movie graphically documents how their love unraveled to the point of destroying each other. An affair, abusive outbursts, blaming, and conflict over their careers all culminate into a bitter divorce battle.

No one goes into marriage thinking they will someday be sitting in a divorce lawyer's office, arguing about child custody and who gets the cat. Nor did any of us envision fifty years of just putting up with each other for the sake of a commitment. How do our genuine feelings of love, appreciation, and longing over time transfer into literally feeling contempt and hatred? How can two people who so optimistically vow to be together for a lifetime experience the gut-wrenching tension of falling out of love?

Yes, there are inevitable bumps along the road like unemployment, infertility, loss, financial stress, and illness, but some couples grow closer during these difficulties while others split apart with the slightest hint of stress. What makes the difference between the two?

People don't come into marriage as blank slates. We are unique individuals carrying wounds, expectations, formative experiences, and personal weaknesses that can complicate the process of navigating the road to intimacy. Marriage doesn't happen in a vacuum. It is deeply impacted by the environment around us and the conflicts within us.

In this chapter, you are going to read about various factors that influence how you and your husband approach marriage, conflict, and difficulty. You might identify with a lot of these obstacles to intimacy and you might feel overwhelmed. Remember that every couple has baggage they bring into marriage. Relationships are just plain hard work but also very much worth the effort. The greatest commandment is about love, loving God and loving each other. Love isn't supposed to be easy. It's okay if your marriage feels more like a hot mess than a hot romance, but I know you don't want to stay there. Working on your marriage can often mean you and your husband are willing to unpack the baggage of pain, fear, and sin you brought with you.

The Past Doesn't Stay in the Past

One of the greatest revelations we experience in the early years of marriage is how much we consider our own upbringing as the normal way of doing things. This is true of little things (like how you celebrate the holidays or what kind of toothpaste you buy) and really significant things (like how you spend money or discipline your children). We naturally assume the way our parents did things is the only way they should be done. The way you respond to conflict, how you handle anger, how much you engage in physical touch, what you do to show love, how much you trust, what you expect your role in the family to be—you began marriage with assumptions about all these things based on how you were raised.

The Impact of Childhood

The effect of the past on the present is enormous. Some Christians are skeptical about counseling approaches that put stock in the power of the past. Yet, God has fearfully and wonderfully created us as complex people with emotions and a brain that records both comforting and traumatic memories. From our childhood experiences, we learn how to deal with stress, how to approach everyday problems, and what we consider normal in relationships.

A trait of childhood is called egocentrism. This means that kids view themselves as the center of the world. In fact, their young world revolves exclusively around them. They have difficulty understanding that anyone else might have emotions and thoughts apart from their own.

I can remember being surprised when I realized that all children did not have the same upbringing that I did. I remember my parents saying, "You are very blessed to have food on the table and parents who love you." When they said these things, I didn't really connect with the truth that other children were growing up without these basic needs being met. Honestly, it probably wasn't until I went away for college or traveled to another country that I truly understood that my worldview and experiences were very different from others.

Through early relationships, we decide if we can trust people and determine if the world basically is a safe or dangerous place.

This childhood egocentric approach means that Mom and Dad and other primary people in a child's life represent the world. Young minds form a basic understanding of themselves and others through their first significant relationships. Our relational "blueprint" is determined by our childhood experiences. Through early relationships, we decide if we can trust people and determine if the world basically is a safe or dangerous place. We also form lasting conclusions about our own worth and value.

Early in my professional career, I worked in an inpatient care center with teenagers who were just out of the juvenile system. On the surface, these teens were rebellious, withdrawn, and often violent. At times, I'd get the opportunity to hear the stories behind their tough veneer. A fifteen-year-old girl told me how she was raised by a mom who was addicted to cocaine. Her mom would sell her for drug money again and again. A seventeen-year-old guy explained how as a young boy, he saw both his father and brother shot in a neighborhood turf war. Then he was tossed from foster home to foster home. Every time he tried to trust someone, he got burned or was abandoned.

These kids graphically displayed how pain and loss from childhood set them up for great difficulties and dysfunction in relationships. Although your story might not be that extreme, you and your husband have experienced things that have deeply impacted your relational worldview.

I've seen this play out in my own marriage. I have a lot to be grateful for in my upbringing. My parents were loving and encouraging and provided for my needs, which gave me a great foundation of trust in my adult relationships. Because of what I experienced growing up, I assume Mike has my best interest at heart and I intuitively know how to depend on him without being needy. But I also brought to marriage the belief that performance equals love.

I was one of six children and often felt like I was competing for my parents' love and attention. I was the conscientious student who cried when I got a B or got caught doing anything wrong. If love could be earned by achievement and obedience, then it could also be lost by failing to live up to a standard.

This core belief fueled much of who I became as a teenager and young adult. I had ulcers because of my fear of disappointing someone. I was driven to not only do my best but to be the best. Although I didn't appear to be a competitive person on the surface, I measured everything and everyone by my performance. I transferred this blueprint onto God, believing that I could earn or lose God's love and approval based on my performance.

I cannot underestimate how much this has impacted my relationships over the years. I realize now that I was attracted to Mike because he didn't have any standards of performance for me. I could relax and have fun with him. But when we got married, I started to feel that Mike should also be the best at everything. He was now a reflection of me. I couldn't see how this belief fueled my pride and my desire to control my husband. At the same time, I had trouble confronting Mike because I didn't want to lose his love. Honestly, I was tied up in knots. Over the years, exposing this pattern has set me free to give and receive genuine love.

What we learn about ourselves and others growing up is difficult to unlearn. Early childhood experiences are stored in the memory with emotions rather than words. A two-year-old doesn't have the words and understanding to remember that Mom yelled all the time, but the experience of feeling unsafe and unloved will be permanently registered.

The Impact of the Teen Years

Adolescence (from about twelve years to twenty years in age) also represents a critical time in a person's development. The foundations of lifetime decisions are usually set in this relatively short period of time. During the teen years both you and your husband began to develop your sense of identity apart from your family. You started to form what have become deeply held beliefs about worth, relationships, and sexuality.

It's interesting to me how many people refer back to rejection and awkwardness of middle or high school when they talk about their current insecurities: "I remember not having anyone to sit with at lunch." "I was the new kid at school and got teased mercilessly." "I'll never forget the humiliation of being cut from the basketball team. I never wanted to put myself out there again."

While these relatively normal growing pains can leave threads of insecurity, more traumatic experiences during the teenage years can be devastating: a date rape, parents' bitter divorce battle, a teen pregnancy, an abusive dating relationship, exposure to pornography or hookups. While childhood trauma leaves a scar, things that happen to a teenager come with the added shame of assumed responsibility, "I should have known better. It's my fault."

> While childhood trauma leaves a scar, things that happen to a teenager come with the added shame of assumed responsibility, "I should have known better. It's my fault."

Noah was almost forty years old when he first verbalized that he had been sexually abused as a young teenager at a youth camp. He remembered the special attention his counselor gave him. He also recalled being asked to do some things that made him feel very uncomfortable, but he'd never considered this to be child abuse. The memories surfaced in marriage counseling as Noah and his wife addressed sexual dysfunction in their marriage. For decades Noah had lived with the unspoken feeling that he had been complicit in what happened at that camp. After all, he had become sexually aroused during the incident and he liked the feelings of being special to the counselor. Didn't this say something about his role in what happened? Even now as a married man, he thought of his sexual desire as twisted and dirty because of what happened when he was thirteen years old.

The teen years can be filled with confusing experiences, poor judgment, and deep wounds. Old enough to make decisions but too young to understand the consequences, these events take root in a person's heart, perpetuating shame and fear.

We all operate with unspoken rules of relationship that we formed through our most formative years: "You just don't talk about those things." "The one who yells the loudest is in charge." "I'll never live up to your expectations." "I must always prove that I'm right in order to be respected." "It's dangerous to be weak. I need to stay in control." As you and your husband navigate the challenges of intimacy, you will often be guided by your unconscious assumptions about how you gain and lose love and how to avoid emotional pain. This leads to the triggers I discussed in the last chapter. Every misunderstanding is laden with fears of repeated patterns from the past. You put on layers of protective armor, sabotaging the possibility of intimacy.

Moving Past the Past

L. T. Holdcroft said it well, "Past experience should be a guide post, not a hitching post." People who perpetually think about the past become victims of it. However, the opposite is also true. Ignoring the effects of the past can equally enslave a person's present decisions. It is vitally important to understand how people and events influenced your life and to become aware of how those experiences affect your current relationships.

If this is not your first marriage, you need to understand how your previous relationships have impacted your view of intimacy and marriage. Without a doubt, you will see your current husband in the light of your former one. You might find yourself repeating destructive patterns or veering to the opposite extreme in this relationship.

> **Unpacking the baggage of your past is a journey, not an event. Think of it as a voyage of curiosity and discovery over time.**

Unpacking the baggage of your past is a journey, not an event. Think of it as a voyage of curiosity and discovery over time. As triggers come up, be curious about them. *"Why did that bother me so much? When did I feel that way before?"* This is not just a psychological exercise; it can be how God exposes the lies that we have believed for many years. It is often how He sets us free.

Journaling, reading, and talking about past experiences can be helpful through this process. When very painful memories are involved, seek the help of a Christian counselor. Discipleship and mentoring are also a great way for couples to learn together. It's one thing to read a book, but it's far more powerful to watch a real-life couple interact with each other. Find a couple who is a few steps ahead of you and whose lives show a strong commitment to God and to marriage. Good mentors will let you know that they don't have it all figured out either, but they can pass down the wisdom God has given them along the way.

Check Your Expectations

Several years ago, our family went on a big trip to Hawaii. We'd saved all our air miles and built the trip up to be a once-in-a-lifetime, epic experience. Our youngest son, Christian, was eleven years old and was excited about this adventure. He had a lot of questions about the long flight to Hawaii. I had never flown to Hawaii but had traveled internationally and assumed it would be a similar experience. I told him that the plane would have a built-in entertainment system in every seat, so he could watch movies, television, or play games. I told him that they would serve us dinner on the plane and there would be lots of snacks. For an eleven-year-old, this sounded even better than playing on a beach in Hawaii!

As we boarded the plane, Christian and I quickly realized that I got it all wrong. The plane had no entertainment—not even movies—for the long voyage. While his brothers brought music and their own games to play, Christian had nothing to do. He packed away all his toys and games expecting to be entertained by the airline. And as far as food? We were offered some crackers and soda to sustain us for the eight-hour flight. Fortunately, my ever-prepared husband shared his trail mix.

Our epic trip to Hawaii was off to a rocky start for young Christian, and his excitement very quickly turned into complaining. I thought about the irony of taking an eleven-year-old kid to Hawaii and hearing him fuss about no game system or airplane meal. But I also realized that I had set him up for this disappointment by building up unrealistic expectations.

Sure enough, our sons had an amazing time despite setbacks like no air-conditioning in the house we rented (in August!), bugs everywhere, and ear infections from swimming. Even a dream vacation will have bumps in the road. It's wise to build that into our expectations!

Most of us have had those moments in marriage where we felt like Christian on the airplane. Throughout your marriage, you are likely to go through seasons where you feel disconnected from your husband, moments when you wished you could get out of your marriage, and even times when you feel attracted to someone else. It's difficult to remember that marriage is a great gift when we run smack up against disappointment.

> Feeling "in love" and feeling close to your husband are not defining qualities of marriage. They are often the *byproduct* but not the *foundation* of a solid marriage.

When you feel this stab of disappointment, you will probably wonder if your marriage is broken. Remember this: feeling "in love" and feeling close to your husband are not defining qualities of marriage. They are often the *byproduct* but not the *foundation* of a solid marriage.

Modern marriages have such unrealistic expectations tied to them that few can live up to the billing. Your spouse will be your sexually compatible best friend and soul mate who shares all your hobbies and interests. You will be different enough to complement each other but alike enough to understand one another. Good luck finding that fairy tale!

Studies have consistently shown that arranged marriages have the same or even higher levels of long-term happiness as free choice marriages.[i] Maybe that is because the husband and wife have more realistic expectations. They hope to *learn to love* rather than expecting to always *feel in love*.

Even the most committed Christian couple finds it difficult to fight the notion that marriage should always include the feelings of love and friendship. Can you find even one marriage in the Bible that is primarily characterized by uninterrupted love and friendship? In the Scriptures, we see husbands and wives working together, serving God together, arguing, and misunderstanding each other. Even in Solomon's erotic book of Songs, the couple is at times working through conflict and disappointment.

In Genesis 24, we see a match literally made in heaven. Abraham sent his servant on a mission to find his son, Isaac, a godly wife. The servant traveled to Abraham's homeland where his journey ended at a well. He prayed for the Lord to make it clear to him the wife He had chosen for Isaac. In walked Rebekah, a direct answer to prayer. This was the woman God had handpicked for Isaac. Sounds like it could be a Disney movie plotline so far, right? Not so fast. The next years are filled with the despair of not having children followed by contention between the two sons God eventually blessed them with. The last recorded scene of Isaac and Rebekah's marriage is them introducing the family themes of favoritism with their sons and plotting against each other. Even a marriage made in heaven turned out to be not quite so romantic!

The bedrock foundation of your marriage can be nothing other than a call to the promise of covenant love. As you likely said in your wedding vows, "For better or for worse. In sickness and in health. For richer or for poorer. Even on bad marriage days, I'll be committed to you."

Your marriage represents your deepest promise to another human being, but that doesn't mean that marriage will meet all your relational, emotional, and spiritual needs. You need other significant relationships with friends, your parents, your small group, and mentors. Most importantly, you need a faith in God that can sustain you through difficult times. Even the best husband will not always reassure you, encourage you, and pull you through every difficulty of life. You are setting your marriage up for failure if you expect your husband to meet needs that only God can meet.

While having unrealistic expectations about marriage is dangerous, so is having no expectations.

While having unrealistic expectations about marriage is dangerous, so is having no expectations. There is a well-known Proverb that says, "Without a vision, the people will perish" (Prov. 29:18 NIV). We need hope and a vision for what marriage can be. On our flight to Hawaii, my son Christian needed to know that eight hours in a plane is not an eternity and that soon we would be having a wonderful time together. He also needed to remember that even though he was disappointed about the flight, it wasn't right to pout or complain. We expected him to have a grateful attitude. In a similar way, healthy expectations for marriage fuel the desire to work through conflict, endure through difficult seasons, and have a thankful spirit even as we may be grieving the loss of something we'd hoped for.

So, what are healthy expectations for your marriage and for your husband?

Expect that marriage will be a journey. There will be ups and downs, highs and lows.

Expect that you and your husband will be honest with each other. Breaches in trust undermine the heart of a covenant and need to be addressed as such.

Expect to treat each other with grace and kindness. Navigating your differences and failures within marriage is impossible without gentleness and forgiveness.

Expect that your marriage will reap what you sow. Although marriage is not a math equation, God has created human relationships to grow with certain behaviors (like humility, kindness, truth, forgiveness) and to die with others (bitterness, selfishness, betrayal). Invest in your marriage, even if the results aren't immediately evident.

In some marriages, even these basic expectations are not met. Maybe you or your husband are not honest, kind, or forgiving. Perhaps the journey of marriage feels like one long trek through an unending valley. You are sowing seeds of prayer, humility, and wisdom but reaping no rewards. Sometimes the wounds and limitations we bring into marriage or our own stubbornness mean that the good seeds we plant bounce right off a hard heart. My friend, if you are in this situation, I understand that you are not just feeling disappointed. You are feeling despair.

I have a young friend who had only been married for four years when her husband abruptly left. I have another dear friend whose husband battled addictions and medical issues for years before he took his own life. I know many men and women who have been faithful, open to counseling, and desperate to work on a marriage but were married to a spouse who consistently refused help and blamed them for their problems.

The Scripture tells us that God is near to the brokenhearted. I believe this promise. I can't tell you what to do in your specific marriage, but I can encourage you to pursue God. Run to Him and He will "guide you and counsel you in the way you should go."ⁱⁱ Seek godly counsel from wise people who uphold the biblical sanctity of marriage but also understand the nuances of how it can become destructive.

Your Flesh Sabotages Love

Sinners make lousy lovers. Unfortunately, we are all sinners. Your childhood and other experiences can explain why you might struggle with anger, lust, or pride but underneath it all is the fact that we don't naturally love one another well.

When I was a young Christian, I tried hard to follow the rules and principles of my faith. I muzzled my jealous thoughts, pressed down my anger, and tried to have a grateful and joyful attitude. It was exhausting and discouraging. No matter how hard I tried, I couldn't muster the kind of love my marriage and friendships required. In weak moments, I found myself saying and doing things I knew were wrong.

Jesus taught that sin is really the overflow of our hearts.[iii] My sin problem is not that I say or do the wrong things; it is rooted in the fact that my heart is sick. I am bent toward rebellion and selfishness, no matter how hard I try to be a good person. Even my efforts at doing the right thing can be rooted in pride. I can feel better than my husband for being more spiritual than he is. I just swap one sin pattern for another.

You don't look at pornography primarily because you have a lust problem. You look at it because you believe that porn is a better salve for your pain than God is. You don't hold on to bitterness because you have an anger problem. You do so because you believe your bitterness is a better way to protect yourself than trusting the Lord. You don't nag your husband because you want to fix him. You do it because you want to be his personal Holy Spirit. You think you can do a better job reforming him than God could do. All this flows from a heart that trusts and worships self more than we trust and worship God.

We are not alone in this desperate battle with sin. The apostle Paul described his frustration and anguish as doing what he promised not to do and failing to do what he knew was the right thing.[iv]

There is one solution to our sin. Death. I'm not talking about physical death, but putting to death your human desires. (The Bible calls this our flesh.) Christianity is not a list of rules to follow. It is the invitation to follow Jesus in death, so that He can live within us, giving us a new heart.

> Christianity is not a list of rules to follow. It is the invitation to follow Jesus in death, so that He can live within us, giving us a new heart.

"By this all people **will know** that **you are my disciples**, if **you** have **love for one another**" (John 13:35 emphasis added).

Spend just a moment thinking about this statement. Of all the things that might mark someone as a follower of Jesus, why is it love? I would expect that Jesus would have mentioned theology, church attendance, or having a "quiet time" as the primary indicators of who were His legitimate followers. But no. Jesus said the defining characteristic of His people would be in how they loved one another.

We fall "out of love" because in our humanity, we only know how to love in a way that is self-centered. I will love as long as you are meeting my needs. I will love you as long as it doesn't require too much of me. This kind of love has limits on what is too great to forgive and what faults are too annoying to tolerate. But Jesus calls us to a different love—an impossible love:

Love is patient. (I'll wait on God and not try to change you.)

Love is kind. (My words will nourish you, not tear you down.)

Love does not envy. (I will not harbor thoughts of wanting what I don't have.)

Love is not proud. (I will honor you as a son of God and someone I can always learn from.)

Love is not rude. (I won't say offensive things.)

Love is not self-seeking. (I won't try to get my way, but I will strive for God's will in our marriage.)

Love is not easily angered. (I will keep short accounts, addressing issues with grace.)

Love keeps no record of wrong. (I will not remind you of ways that you've hurt me or nurture bitterness in my heart.)

Love does not delight in evil. (I will humbly confront you when you sin and expect you to do the same for me. I want to pursue God's righteousness together.)

Love rejoices with the truth. (I will rejoice when we can be honest with each other and when the truth of God sets us free.)

Love always trusts. (I will trust in your heart, even if we are in a difficult season of marriage.)

Love always protects. (I've got your back. You can trust me to not willfully hurt you.)

Love always hopes. (I choose to see the best in you and place my hope in a God who never fails.)

Love always perseveres. (When our marriage is exhausting and disappointing, I will keep my eyes fixed on Jesus. I won't give up on you or us.)

Love never fails. (I won't bail on you when things get difficult. I won't stop loving you even when I no longer feel in love.)

Imagine if those were your wedding vows. Could you promise before God to love your husband like that? I couldn't. Genuine love is supernatural. Our human "wifely" love has a shelf life, especially when marriage gets difficult. Jesus also said that even pagans know how to love people who are kind to them.[v] But only through God can our love overcome our self-interest. This kind of pure love is only possible through the work of Jesus Christ in your life, through Him living in and through you.

Marriage is such a great invitation to display God's love because it invites us to love in a way that doesn't simply satisfy our fleshly desires but transcends them.

One of my favorite authors, Andrew Murray, wrote, "Your (Christian) life is every day to be a proof that God works impossibilities; your (Christian) life is to be a series of impossibilities made possible and actual by God's almighty power."[vi] Friend, what I want you to understand is that a godly marriage isn't simply difficult. It's impossible. An impossibility made possible by God.

God, Help Us!

Because I am trained in psychology, I can give you loads of advice on how to address wounds from your past and how to communicate with your husband. As helpful as psychological advice might be, it cannot ultimately conquer that which plagues your marriage. Even our emotional wounds from the past have such power because they camp out as patterns of sin and self-protection.

You may have grown up in a chaotic and abusive home. In an effort to deal with your pain and anxiety, you developed strategies to control your environment. That's psychology. But when your husband or mentor points out that you are controlling, you get defensive and refuse to change. That's a stronghold of sin.

I shared earlier with you about the patterns of competitiveness and pride that coursed through my heart because of my insecurities about love. I understood why I was so fearful of losing love, but I still couldn't stop my jealous feelings when someone else succeeded. Even while doing ministry, I deeply longed to be admired and feared messing up. I put pressure on my husband and kids to be perfect because they reflected me. Many of the spiritual things I did were rooted in trying to earn God's love and approval, and I knew it.

A good psychologist could help me understand this, but only the Healer could release me from it. Jesus died to set me free, so how could I be free? I spent a lot of years in marriage tinkering with different strategies. Some worked and some didn't. I rode the roller coaster of good seasons and bad ones. Although I learned how to become a good wife, the rivers of my selfishness, insecurities, and pride were still there.

About fifteen years into my marriage, the Lord began to do a deep work within me. Surrender. Instead of trying to fix myself and fix my marriage, I learned to daily come to the Lord empty with open hands. It's changed my life, and it's changed my marriage.

The question is this: What is more important? Staying safe and in control or becoming a woman who is literally a "new creation in Christ" with a new heart and the supernatural capacity to love?

I remember meeting with a woman who insisted that her marriage was hopeless. Over the course of many meetings, she learned how her own sin and choices were contributing to the destructive pattern. She insisted over and over that she was unable to change. Our work together ended when she admitted that it was not a matter of ability but a matter of will. One of Satan's most seductive traps is convincing us that we *cannot* do what we *will not* do.

Over the past years, I have witnessed some truly miraculous changes in marriages. When it comes down to it, God can radically change lives! He can tear down walls of anger, guilt, and fear if you surrender to Him.

You may be a Christian, but have you asked God to truly give you a new heart? Again, I will quote Andrew Murray from his life-changing book, *Absolute Surrender*:

> The cause of the weakness of your Christian life is that you want to work it out partly and to let God help you. And that cannot be. You must come to be utterly helpless, to let God work, and God will work gloriously. . . . Have you said, "In worship, in work, in sanctification, in obedience to God, I can do nothing of myself, and so my place is to worship the omnipotent God, and to believe that he will work in me every moment?" Oh, may God teach us this![vii]

We all have a cocktail of painful experiences, expectations, and sin patterns that will sabotage our attempts at love. When we understand this, we see that it is really a miracle for two people to learn to love each other well—not just tolerate each other—over a lifetime. The good news is that this is a miracle God desires to do in your marriage.

Endnotes

i   https://www.psychologytoday.com/us/blog/the-science-love/201208/ arranged-vs-love-based-marriages-in-the-us-how-different-are-they.

ii Psalm 32:8.

iii Luke 6:45.

iv See Romans 7.

v　See Matthew 5:46–48.

vi　Andrew Murray, *Humility & Absolute Surrender* (Peabody, MA: Hendrickson Publisher. 2005). 112.

vii　Murray, *Humility & Absolute Surrender,* pp. 113–114.

Chapter 9

learning to make love

Growing up in a Christian family, I didn't hear much about sex. I knew that it was important to save it for marriage and that it was supposed to be frequent and fun once we said, "I do." It didn't take long into my honeymoon to realize that sex was not exactly the gift I was hoping for. Honestly, I could have done without it.

Sex was painful for me, and I didn't know why. I gathered up the courage to ask my ob-gyn. She said everything looked fine. I just needed to relax. How do you relax when something hurts?

I wish I could say that Mike and I quickly outgrew these challenges, but sex remained one of the greatest sources of disappointment and conflict in our marriage for many years. It was actually one of the last things I wanted to talk about as a psychologist.

When I wrote the first version of this book, the chapter on sex was at the end of the book and called "No More Headaches." I reluctantly wrote it because you can't write a marriage book without having a chapter on sex. Then women's groups started contacting me to speak on that chapter. There were so few women (especially Christian women) willing to talk about the topic that I was considered an expert because I wrote a chapter on it!

A few years later, I wrote an entire book by that title. Why? Because so many women resonated with my frustration and disappointment around sexual intimacy. Many of the challenges in that book represented my own pain. The best advice that I had for both myself and for my readers was to approach this area of marriage with a willingness to confront challenges. While I would still give some of that same advice, there is a deeper understanding of the gift of sexuality that I didn't grasp back then.

I really like jigsaw puzzles, but I would never want to attempt one without having the picture on the front of the box. Whenever I try to figure out where a piece belongs, I compare it to that picture. Your sex life is like a 2,000-piece jigsaw puzzle; it's complicated with a lot of pieces that don't seem to fit together. But the challenge of sexual intimacy is nearly impossible if you don't know the picture sex is intended to create. What should your sex life *look like*?

Most women have no idea why sex is important in marriage and have even less of a clue as to why it might be important to God. They have learned from movies and our modern culture that sex is all about self-fulfillment. The church countered that message by emphasizing "sexual purity" above all else. Neither of those narratives helps couples navigate through seasons of disappointment and conflict.

I'd like to suggest to you what is on the front of the box of that jigsaw puzzle. If you have the context for why sex is so powerful, so vulnerable, and often so disappointing, it will give you a completely different perspective on how and why to make it a priority in your marriage.

Sex and the Big Picture

One day, my teenage son asked me, "Mom, where does the Bible say we shouldn't have sex before marriage?" I could have explained to my son the meaning of the Greek words *fornication* and *sexual immorality* in the many Bible passages that tell us what *not* to do with our sexuality. Instead, I explained to him the concept of covenant love. I don't believe that God's rules about sexuality are arbitrary but are connected to the mystery of His divine purposes.

The overarching theme of the Bible is God's pursuit and redemption of His people. Author and teacher Christopher West explains it this way: "The Bible can be summed up in five words: God wants to marry us."[i] From the very beginning of Genesis to the very end of Revelation, we see that God created male and female, the covenant promise of marriage, and the sexual union of husband and wife to be not only sacred but symbolic. I've alluded to this in earlier chapters, but it's critical to also make the connection as it relates to sexual intimacy in marriage.

You might be able to accept (even if you don't fully understand) that your marriage somehow represents God's love for His covenant people, but applying that to sex seems a bit farfetched and maybe even cringey. One comedian put it this way: "To hear many religious people talk, one would think God created the torso, head, legs and arms, but the Devil slapped on the genitals."[ii] This separation of God and sexuality is part of many church traditions, but I assure you it's not biblical. God's Word talks about sex *a lot*, and not just in reference to what not to do. The entire book of the Song of Solomon is a celebration of passionate sex between a husband and wife. The Old

It should actually feel unnatural to think about sex apart from thinking about God.

Testament is filled with stories about sexuality. The prophets continually used sexual terms to describe God's covenant love with Israel and their unfaithfulness to Him.

It should actually feel unnatural to think about sex *apart from thinking about God*. I love how Matt Chandler describes it,

> God put the penis on the man, and he put the testicles on the man, and he filled those testicles with sperm. He created all tissue—some that would expand, some that would secrete; he filled the man with testosterone that would drive much of his life. From the beginning, this was God's idea. . . . And he shaped the woman differently, he gave her larger breasts, rounder hips, and a vagina. He filled the woman with a different hormone, estrogen. The woman's body was not the Devil's idea; it was all God's doing.[iii]

So, what exactly *was* God doing when He created us as sexual people, male and female? Why did He make sex so powerful, so intimate, so vulnerable, and so complicated? Because with our sexuality, He was giving us an earthy picture of the nature of His love.

If you do not see this as the backdrop to your sexuality, you will be continually confused and frustrated (as I was) in trying to make sense of sex in your marriage. God may seem cruel and unloving as you walk through seasons of pain, unmet longings, and seemingly biblically based demands that meet your husband's sexual needs and ignore your own. Understanding the purpose of sexuality and sexual intimacy in marriage will completely transform how you approach everything from sexual pleasure to sexual betrayal.

Sex Celebrates and Cements Your Covenant

Let's break down three words from this heading: *covenant, celebrates,* and *cements.* I've used this word *covenant* many times already, but I don't want to assume you understand exactly what it means. After all, where do you hear the word *covenant* in normal conversation?

A covenant is a unique type of relationship. Most relationships we have with people are contractual. You relate to someone because they benefit you and you benefit them. This obviously applies to business relationships but also friendships. Although you and your best friend didn't sign a contract agreeing to what you bring to each other, your relationship is based on a number of unspoken assumptions like: "You'll respond to me when I text you." "I can call you if I'm having a rough day." "We will hang out about once a month." "You will have my back even when we disagree." When you or your friend breaks one of these unspoken rules, your relationship might even end. Friends come and go based on whether or not we are meeting one another's needs in a given season.

A covenant is different because it's based on a promise. If you parented your children with a "contract" mindset, you would be a terrible parent. Imagine if you told your one-year-old child, "You are not allowed to wake me up in the middle of the night, nor are you allowed to throw a temper tantrum. If you do these things, I'm not going to be your mom anymore." You faithfully love your children even when they are disobedient and rebellious and when you feel like walking out on them. God says that He is like this good parent who loves us with that type of unconditional love.

While the parent-child relationship is an important covenant, the marriage relationship is even more significant. Why? Because you must choose to love not based on your husband's need or what feels good, but based on your character. You can't realistically walk away from your children, but you can walk away from your husband.

We save sex for marriage because sex is the *celebration* of this holy covenant promise between a man and a woman. It is the physical expression of the choice to join two lives together for a lifetime. Sex is the party that celebrates the promise. This is why sex was created to be pleasurable. When a couple has good sex, powerful chemicals, like the neurotransmitter dopamine, are released into the brain. Sex is not about reasoning or thinking. It involves an uninhibited giving and receiving of passion and pleasure.

If I had read this last sentence twenty years ago, I would have thought, "Well that's not been my experience." I've learned over years of ministry that many women would say the same thing. In fact, some have just settled for a sexless marriage or a sex life without passion and pleasure.

> While sex may not always be passionate and pleasurable, this is a worthy goal to work toward because it is the expression of a true celebration.

Let me be very clear about this. Your marriage is not dependent on a great sex life. Your marriage is at heart a covenant. But God has given you and your husband the gift of sex to remember and celebrate that covenant. While sex may not always be passionate and pleasurable, this is a worthy goal to work toward because it is the expression of a true celebration. Sexual passion and pleasure in marriage matter, not because it is an end in itself, but because of the covenant it celebrates.

God has also created sexual intimacy to be a physical bond that *cements* your covenant promise. This was a huge ah-ha moment for me in discovering why a regular sex life is an important part of a healthy marriage. It also helped me understand why sex matters a lot to my husband.

When we have sex, our bodies secrete the hormone oxytocin. That hormone will probably sound familiar to you if you've had children. Oxytocin is a key hormone to induce labor, breastfeeding, and the powerful bonding that happens between a woman and her child. Adult females produce oxytocin throughout daily life but get massive doses of it during pregnancy, delivery, and after having a child. Oxytocin has been nicknamed the "cuddle hormone" and "love hormone" because it gives you rose-colored glasses, creating positive feelings when your brain is flooded with it. God is a genius. How else could a woman endure sleepless nights, the piercing scream, and absolute dependency of her newborn? Amazingly, women not only care for their young children but form a deep, enduring attachment even though the baby has nothing to offer!

As a woman, you also experience oxytocin rushes when you connect meaningfully with friends or with your husband. Men are impacted by oxytocin and a closely related hormone, vasopressin. They experience small amounts when they play with their child or hold their wife's hand, but they only get the big rush of this hormone during and after sex. Some studies show that men experience increasingly more oxytocin (think bonding) and less testosterone (think aggressive or competitive behavior) the longer they are in a committed relationship.[iv]

Has your husband ever said, "Sex makes me feel close to you"? This is literally true! Some researchers call oxytocin the fidelity hormone because its presence has been proven to deter men from moving toward other women.[v]

This information is not to pile guilt on you if your sex life feels completely absent or broken. I also recognize that in many marriages, sex doesn't seem to be important to the man. Even so, here's the takeaway: God has created sex to be a very powerful, intimate way that you and your husband remember and reinforce your promise to one another. Even our biology affirms this design. The neurotransmitters and hormones released during sex were created to form long-term attachments even within your brain!

Sex Tests and Refines Your Love

When speaking to college-age women about God's design for sexuality, I'm often asked, "How do you know if you're sexually compatible if you don't have sex before you get married?" This question reveals a fundamental misunderstanding on what's "on the front of the box," not only of sex, but also of marriage.

God did not create marriage so that you would be continually satisfied with your soul mate. There is a certain amount of natural frustration and incompatibility built into marriage (and sex) no matter who you marry. Mix that with selfishness and pride and you have a recipe for ongoing conflict. God created marriage (including sex) to teach us to love the way He loves us.

In the early years of my marriage, I believed that the hardships and conflicts Mike and I had around sex were a great barrier to our love. In fact, I determined the first questions I would ask God when I got to heaven would be, "Why did you make me and my husband so different sexually? Why did you give us this 'gift' without the ability to enjoy it? God, I feel as if this was a cruel joke." Most of the couples I've talked to have echoed this frustration at some point in their marriage. Their bodies don't work the way they should. They are riddled with insecurity and shame about sex. One of them has no desire for sex or can't experience pleasure.

While many of these frustrations are the result of living in a fallen world, men and women were different even before sin marred the human experience. Just look at this chart reflecting on some fundamental differences in the ways that the average man and woman are wired sexually:

Basic Sexual Differences Between Men and Women[vi]

MEN	WOMEN
Sex leads to feelings of love	Feelings of love leads to sex
Quickly aroused and satisfied	Slowly aroused and satisfied
Best part of sex is **release** tension—the goal	Best part of sex is **buildup** of tension—the journey
Wants immediate direct stimulation in one place	Wants to be touched everywhere—delaying direct stimulation
Wants sex in order to relax	Must relax in order to have sex
Aroused visually	Aroused by emotions/ sensations
Sexual prime— late teens, early 20s	Sexual prime— 30s and 40s
Desire dependent on constant hormone	Desire dependent on changing hormones
Capable of single orgasm	Capable of multiple and varied orgasms

I believe that these differences likely existed with Adam and Eve before sin entered the world. God made you and your husband sexually different not to frustrate you, but because *differences create a bridge that only love can cross.* Think of it this way. Imagine that you and your husband had exactly the same sexual needs and always wanted sex the same way at the same time of day. You never fought about sex. You never needed to talk about it because you instinctively always had the same desires. On the surface, you might think, *That would be heaven!* But what would get lost in the absence of navigating sexual differences?

God has created the sexual relationship so that it's absolutely impossible for a husband and wife to have a long-term fulfilling sex life without learning to love each other.

God has created the sexual relationship so that it's absolutely impossible for a husband and wife to have a long-term fulfilling sex life without learning to love each other. No matter how compatible you might seem, the years and stress of marriage will bring out incompatibilities and conflicts that tap into pride, fear, and selfishness.

When my children were young, I highly valued my evenings. As much as I loved them, I saw bedtime as an anticipated finish line every night. A relaxing evening for me did not include mustering the energy for sex and having to share my body with yet another person. I felt like I had earned me time. As a spiritual woman, I made sure that my evenings included my Bible, devotional, and cup of tea. Sometimes, I'd get annoyed if Mike interfered with my time alone with God.

I remember one evening reading my Bible and praying very earnestly, "God, I want to love you more deeply. Show me how to surrender more of my life for you." You never know how God might answer that kind of dangerous prayer! The Holy Spirit responded to my prayer in a totally unexpected way.

"Juli, you can begin by loving your husband well." I knew this

was about the fact that I had been avoiding sex in our marriage.

"But Lord," I said, "you wouldn't want me to cut short my quiet time!"

God is far more concerned with your love life than He is with your sex life.

There are times when God asks us to stop hiding, even behind spiritual things, to show His love, not just study it. In this season of my marriage, this is what God was asking me to do.

Here's the point. God is far more concerned with your love life than He is with your sex life. He will use the very things that frustrate you to challenge you and your husband to love each other more deeply.

God's love for you cost Him something. Jesus gave His life to be reunited with His bride. If marriage and sex are metaphors of this, why would the metaphor not also include elements of sacrificial love? Yes, our sin and our husbands' sin contribute greatly to our sexual brokenness. But redemption means God is able to transform beauty out of ashes and praise out of despair.

I don't know what disappointment, hurt, shame, and betrayal you are facing in your sexual relationship with your husband right now. But God can use these very things to teach you a deeper form of love and intimacy. I think of the many couples I've talked to over the years who demonstrate this truth. One is Katie and Jake.

Katie was physically, emotionally, and sexually abused throughout her childhood. During their fifteen years of marriage, she and her husband have experienced long stretches during which sex was not even possible. Any touching resulted in flashbacks and panic attacks. Even now, the prospect of a thriving sex life seems like a distant dream.

When I talked to Jake about this situation, he readily admitted the frustration of being cheated out of a healthy sex life in his marriage. Both he and his wife had envisioned sex as a fun and bonding experience in their marriage. This great evil that was done to Katie has robbed them both, and they are rightfully angry and disappointed. But Jake has a choice. He can either seek sexual fulfilment somewhere else or choose to view their marriage through the lens of the front of the puzzle box. He can deny his wife or deny himself, leaning into the call to love Katie as Christ loves the church and gave Himself up for her. Many of Jake's friends would understand if he got his needs met through porn or even wanted to leave his marriage. Yet he has the opportunity to even more fully experience what marriage was created to be. Far more than a husband who experiences sexual satisfaction, this man can choose to walk in the depth of a Jesus who gave Himself fully to love His bride.

Katie can also make the choice to love. Her past trauma has severely limited her ability to engage in sexual intimacy with her husband. But she can either stay stuck as a victim or courageously walk the long journey of healing. It will take time, but God can heal her memories.

I have seen husbands and wives at every stage of marriage respond to heartbreaking challenges with the choice to press deeper into loving each other and learning to rebuild trust because they see the bigger picture.

A lot of religious teaching about sex in the church emphasizes the need for singles to abstain from sex and build character through self-control. The unspoken (and sometimes spoken) message is that once you get married, you can experience sex without any need for self-discipline or patience. "Just wait for marriage and it will be great!" Getting married may be the finish line for one form of sexual purity, but it is also the starting line for new ways that God wants to refine your character and teach you the nature of genuine love. God is always working.

> Getting married may be the finish line for one form of sexual purity, but it is also the starting line for new ways that God wants to refine your character and teach you the nature of genuine love.

When I think of all the pain that sex has represented for me as a wife, I chuckle to think that this is the ministry God has called me to. I don't want to reexperience some of the things Mike and I have walked through, but I also see how the valleys were the very places where we learned the meaning of love, mercy, forgiveness, empathy, and intimacy. God will never waste pain that is yielded to Him...even pain from the bedroom.

Relentlessly Address Barriers

An engaged couple asked me, "What should we expect our sex life to be like?" The first words out of my mouth were "You should expect that you will run into some challenges." I didn't leave them with this depressing news. I shared with them the wonders and joys of sex in marriage, but I wanted them to be prepared.

In the pursuit of sexual intimacy, *every couple* will encounter obstacles. Some of those barriers will be small, but others will be profound.

Zack and Josie have been trying to conceive for over three years. Every month is met with disappointment. Last year, they took a loan to try in vitro fertilization. Josie got pregnant with twins, which she miscarried in the second trimester. Sex is no longer about fun or intimacy. It represents heartbreak.

Morgan grew up in a very conservative Christian culture. She didn't learn much about sex, other than not to do it until she got married. When she first saw porn as a young teenager, she felt ashamed at how her body responded. For the next ten years, she cycled through seasons of fantasy and masturbation followed by shame. When she and Andy got married, she couldn't respond sexually without thinking about sexual images and fantasies she knew were wrong. Yet she couldn't admit to her husband the "dirty" thoughts she had about sex.

Jessica and Matt had a great sex life during the first two years of their relationship. As Christians, they felt guilty about living together and sleeping together, so they got married. After that, everything seemed to unravel. Jessica felt unwanted and unloved as Matt spent more time nurturing his startup business. To get his attention, Jessica had an affair. Once she realized how devastated her husband was, she desperately wanted to fix their marriage. But how do you rewind history?

I could tell you more stories about sexual trauma, betrayal, body parts not working like they should, and sexual shame. There are so many ways that sexual intimacy can be derailed. Even seemingly minor issues like fatigue, low libido, or poor body image can be enough to shut down a love life for decades.

If I were to tackle all the obstacles that couples face in building sexual intimacy, this book would be too heavy to pick up. These barriers can be extremely complicated and excruciating for the couples walking through them. I run a ministry, Authentic Intimacy, which helps encourage women and couples to embrace God's design for sexuality. Practically every week we hear from men and women expressing desperation because of the sexual pain and brokenness they are navigating. While there is not enough space in this book to specifically address the issues I've mentioned, I can give you some guiding principles.

Remember That You're Not Alone

I was meeting with a small group of women who all had significant challenges in their marriages. One young woman who was in the throes of recovering from her husband's affair said, "I know I shouldn't feel this way, but it just helps me knowing that I'm not the only one going through something like this." Although the couples around you look like they have it all together, trust me...many of them have unspoken pain just as you have.

Sexual struggles and sin tend to make us feel isolated. Satan feeds on that by keeping us quiet, afraid to speak the truth and reach out for comfort. He whispers in your ear, "Look at all the beautiful, happy women around you. None of them have the problems you do. You will never be like them. There's no hope for *your* marriage."

People know the focus of my ministry, so they often trust me with their secrets and questions. I promise you, there is more pain around you than you can imagine. Your neighbor or coworker's secret struggles may be different than yours, but find common ground in your need for God's comfort and wisdom. Look for women and couples who are willing to be honest about their struggles and seek God together.

Pray to the Healer

When is the last time you prayed to God specifically about your sex life? When have you and your husband prayed together about this area of your marriage? If you are like most Christian women, you'd probably admit that you have never done this.

Christians feel comfortable praying about cancer, allergies, and even an upset stomach. But few of us are willing to pray:

❦ "God, please help my body to respond sexually to my husband!"

❦ "Please help me stand against the lies I believe about my body!"

❦ "Please help me to heal from these flashbacks I have so that I can be fully present when I have sex with my husband."

❦ "God, bring to light everything that my husband and I need to confess to you and to each other. Help us not to hide in shame."

❦ "Lord, I don't have the strength to forgive him. I can't forgive him for touching her and looking at her. I need your help to put this marriage back together!"

❦ "God, I confess my sexual sin. Forgive me and set me free from the cloud of shame that hovers over me."

If your sex life is truly a spiritual battlefield, how do you expect to win if God is kept at arm's length?

As a psychologist, I understand the importance of science and wholeheartedly encourage counseling. But here's the truth. A counselor cannot heal you. There is One Healer and His name is Jesus. The best counselor or friend will lovingly and skillfully draw you to His presence. God deeply cares about your pain. He wants to remove your shame. As Jesus said, "If the Son sets you free, you will be free indeed!"[vii]

Seek Wise Counsel

One evening after a speaking event, a woman timidly shared with me, "My husband and I have been married for twenty years.

I've never told anyone this, but I can't have an orgasm. Is there any hope?"

Asking a stranger a question like this takes a lot of courage. How many women were at the same event with similar questions but went home without getting such specific help? While there are a lot of frustrating barriers to sexual intimacy, there is also a lot of help available from Christian books, podcasts, sermon series, retreats, sex therapists, and counselors. (See the Resources section in the back of the book for more information.)

Some of the challenges you and your husband are facing in intimacy require specific expertise and knowledge. Here are a few examples:

Sexual Addiction: Saying no to porn and other sexual temptations is not always just about will power and prayer. Brain science has revealed that pornography creates powerful pathways in the brain that alter a person's sexual response. Overcoming consistent sexual temptation means that you and your husband need to be connected with Christians who specialize in sexual addiction recovery.

Trauma recovery: Brain science has also demonstrated that abuse and sexual trauma leaves unseen scars. When we experience something traumatic, our bodies become flooded with adrenaline and the memory is uniquely imprinted in the amygdala. When trauma happens repeatedly or in childhood, the brain may protect itself by splitting off memories from our awareness. The effect of abuse and sexual trauma is far-reaching and impacts emotional health, relationship dynamics, and sexual response. If this is your or your husband's story, please seek the help of a Christian counselor who specializes in trauma.

Sexual disorders: There are a variety of things that can go wrong physically with our bodies, including erectile dysfunction, premature ejaculation, pain during sex, inability to become aroused, and not being able to climax. Your ob-gyn is not likely trained to address any of these complaints. Fortunately, there is a growing field of Christian sex therapists and pelvic floor therapists who can help.

Recovering from infidelity: I met with a woman who had discovered two months earlier that her husband had cheated on her with a good friend. Although she was devastated, she just wanted to forgive him and move on. As she shared this story over lunch and asked my advice, I gave her some sobering news. "If you try to forgive and move on too quickly, his sin and your wound will not be adequately addressed to truly heal your relationship."

While I've known many couples who have healed from infidelity, I don't know anyone who has done so quickly. God speaks so strongly against adultery for a reason. It breaks a covenant. Just as in grief, there are stages of recovery for couples who are walking through the wake of betrayal. Make sure you are connected with a counselor or resources that can help you do this well.

The couples that have the greatest sexual intimacy have determined to see a potential victory in the face of each challenge.

Sexual intimacy is a journey. Different stages of that journey will look unique, depending on what obstacles you and your husband may be facing. Don't give up on the journey! God can use any obstacle as an invitation to deeper intimacy. The couples that have the greatest sexual intimacy have determined to see a potential victory in the face of each challenge.

Make Sure You Play Offense

The vast majority of Christian teaching around sex focuses on playing defense: how to say no to temptation, keeping singles sexually pure, and protecting marriages from infidelity. When we play defense, we react to fear. Yes, there are some realistic reasons to fear. If you take seriously what Peter wrote, "The devil is a roaring lion, seeking for someone to devour,"[viii] you will have a healthy fear of you or your husband becoming his prey. But the Scripture also tells us that we were not given a spirit of fear, but one of power, love, and a sound mind.[ix] This is why it is important for every married couple to play offense. When we focus on offense, we are not reacting to what can go wrong but proactively pursuing what is right.

Learn How to Say "Yes"

One of the most common questions women ask is "How do I learn to say 'yes' to sexual pleasure (offense) after years of thinking that sexual pleasure is wrong?" How can a woman's body, soul, and mind make the dramatic shift once sex has now become a good thing?

Sexual intimacy was created to be fully integrated into the choice you make as a bride to unite your life with your husband. When you have sex, you are celebrating with your body what you have chosen to do with the rest of your life. Just as you said "yes" in your vows, you say "yes" over and over again in your bedroom. Sexual intimacy was created to be a mutual "yes." Simply giving your husband sex to meet his needs is not the fullness of God's plan for your sex life. God created for sex to be pleasurable for both of you. Some women (I'll include myself here) have to work at it for sex to be enjoyable in marriage.

Your brain must give your body permission to become sexually aroused.

Sex experts will tell you that your most powerful sexual organ is your brain. Your body is much more likely to respond to thoughts than to touch. Your brain must give your body permission to become sexually aroused. Understanding this has been extremely helpful to me in my own personal journey. What I've realized over the years is that I had set up unconscious stop signs on the mental pathway to sexual pleasure.

Here are some of my old stop signs:

- What if it hurts?
- What if my husband isn't thinking about me?
- I'm not sure I want to do this.
- I don't want to lose control and look stupid.
- What if the kids hear what we are doing?
- Is God really okay with us doing this specific sexual act?

I've had to learn to mentally tear down those stop signs and replace them with green lights that encourage me to "go."

Rather than get frustrated when my body seems to shut down, I've learned to engage my mind. Sometimes I pray, "Lord, you want me to fully enjoy this time with my husband. Will you please help me embrace the freedom to let go and enter into this pleasure?" Other times, I tell myself, "I want this. This is good. I choose to enjoy my husband's touch."

Author's note: If playing offense is a struggle for you, check out a ten-week Bible study I wrote with Linda Dillow called *Passion Pursuit*. We also have Java with Juli podcast episodes, blogs, and other resources that can be helpful at *authenticintimacy.com*.

Make Time for Sex

When I've given women the advice to schedule sex, they often reply, "Well, that's not very romantic!" Honestly, how often does great, spontaneous sex happen in your marriage?

Scheduling sex (or at least setting the expectation for how often you want to have it and who will initiate) gives both you and your husband time to plan and prepare. When sex just happens, usually one of you is tired or distracted. It's often at the end of a long, busy day and all you have to offer each other is whatever is left over. If sexual intimacy is a priority, you will proactively save your best for each other.

This is really important for women who struggle to mentally engage in sex after an exhausting day. A group of Christian psychologists who studied women and sex found "one of the most important indicators of sexual desire is the frequency with which one thinks about sex....In general, the majority of women (43 percent) tend to think about sex once a week, about as often as or little more frequently than they actually have sex. Men tend to think about sex on a daily basis, usually much more frequently than they have sex." (*Secrets of Eve,* p. 62).[x] This is why my husband loves it when I'm writing a book on sex—I'm thinking about it all day!

Making time for sex will look different in unique seasons of marriage. Whether you are juggling the demands of young children or need to plan sex around physical limitations, a good sex life will require intentionality. I know couples who literally sit down with a calendar and plan time to be intimate together. Other couples have standing dates like every Friday night and Sunday morning will be our time together. Sometimes you need more flexibility because of the unpredictability of children, health, or work schedules. In this situation, you might develop a cue that basically means "Let's find a time to be together in the next twenty-four hours." For a while

Mike and I used the cue "requisition order" (I know...doesn't sound very romantic...but it had a secret meaning for us). We also learned to schedule sex before and after either one of us was traveling out of town—the best defense against temptation can be a good offense.

Finding a way to regularly schedule times to be intimate keeps you on offense. Remember that we always make time for the things we value. This means that we may also have to say "no" to other things so that we can say "yes" to sexual intimacy. Say "no" to getting lost in your social media feed or bingeing the latest Netflix series. Say "no" to the dogs or kids sleeping in your bed. Maybe even occasionally say "no" to your early morning workout or your coffee routine.

Let Go of Perfection

It has often been said that perfection is the enemy of the good. I've seen this play out in far too many marriages. You won't let your husband see your naked body because of your physical flaws. You can't enjoy sex with your husband because you have an unresolved conflict. You won't allow yourself to experience sexual pleasure because of your past mistakes. You think your sex life is horrible because it doesn't compare to some romantic fantasy in your head.

These are all ways that the enemy camps out in your mind and discourages you from enjoying the gift God has given you and your husband.

One of the things that truly was a shock to me was learning that God is actually glorified when my husband and I experience sexual pleasure together, even in our imperfection. Let me explain how I learned this.

Not long after writing the book *No More Headaches,* my friend and mentor Linda Dillow (coauthor of the bestselling book

Intimate Issues) asked me if I had ever read the Song of Solomon. Of course I had, but I wrote it off as a poetic book that I couldn't quite connect with. All the symbolism of the garden, the deer, and the pomegranates didn't mean a lot to me. Linda then encouraged me to reread the book with some understanding of what those symbols mean (most of them are sexually related) and to specifically ask the question, "What can I learn from the bride in the Song of Solomon?" When I completed this assignment, my eyes were opened to the idea that this ancient woman was *really into* sex in her marriage. She overcame insecurities about her body and learned to think erotically about her husband. Song of Solomon 5:10–16 is poetry describing the beauty of her husband's naked body, including an ivory tusk—I wonder what that was! (I'm not making this up. The English translators toned down the original words to spare us embarrassment.)

Perhaps the most astonishing and powerful passage in the Song of Solomon is at the end of Chapter 4 where the husband and wife are naked and appear to be in the middle of enjoying each other sexually.

The wife says, "Awake, O north wind, and come, O south wind! Blow upon my garden (this is referring to her genitalia), let its spices flow. Let my beloved come to his garden, and eat its choicest fruits."

The husband says, "I came to my garden, my sister, my bride, I gathered my myrrh with my spice, I ate my honeycomb with my honey, I drank my wine with my milk." In other words, "That was awesome!"

Then in that same verse, the "chorus" responds with encouragement, "Eat, friends, and be drunk with love."

Who does the chorus represent? Who would inspire this husband and wife to be intoxicated by the pleasures of their sexual love? This is not the devil's encouragement or the world's counsel. It is the encouragement of the Creator who designed sexual pleasure to celebrate the deepest of loves. Remember that Solomon and his bride represent an imperfect couple, with physical, relational, and emotional flaws. Yet, God blessed their sexual union.

God is saying, "This is good! This is what I created sexual pleasure for. Enjoy it together to the fullest." My friend, God gives that same encouragement and blessing over you and your husband when you experience sexual pleasure together! Pursuing sexual intimacy is not only how we play offense in our marriage but also how we invite God to reclaim the beauty of sexuality.

How you and your husband navigate your sexual relationship is precious and sacred ground. These earthly bodies are temporary and limited, but what a wonder that God has given us within our bodies the capacity to experience oneness, not just physically, but spiritually and relationally!

Endnotes

i   Java with Juli podcast, episode #313, "The Greatest Love Story." Released June 2020.

ii   Attributed to Don Schrader.

iii   Matt Chandler, *The Mingling of Souls : God's Design for Love, Sex, Marriage, and Redemption* (Colorado Springs, CO: David C Cook, 2014), 13.

iv   https://sciencenordic.com/denmark-mens-health-videnskabdk/marriage-reduces-testosterone-in-men/1445183.

v   https://healthland.time.com/2013/11/27/how-oxytocin-makes-men-almost-monogamous/.

vi   This graph appeared in *Passion Pursuit*, by Linda Dillow and Juli Slattery, published by Moody in 2013.

vii   John 8:36.

viii   I Peter 5:8.

ix   2 Timothy 1:7.

x   Archibald Hart, Catherine Hart Weber, and Debra Taylor, *Secrets of Eve* Word Publishing, 1998.

♥

Chapter 10

your hero in your home

It had been a grueling weekend. I had participated in an out-of-town conference and given seven presentations over the three days of the event. Then, my flight from Portland back to Ohio got canceled. The next morning, my coworker, Kristi, and I caught an early flight home. Even with the early start, the time change and connections made it a long day, and I didn't walk through my front door until around 8:00 PM on Monday night. I breathed a sigh of relief. I was greeted by my dogs, hugged my husband and son, got some of my favorite snacks from our pantry, and then slept in my own bed. Home is restful. Home means I can be quiet (I'm an introvert). Home is where I recharge.

Does home feel this way for you? Perhaps when you walk through your door, you tense, preparing for conflict. And how about your husband? For many men, home is not a place of emotional respite but an environment filled with emotional land mines. Remember, people like to spend time where they feel wanted, useful, respected, and capable. Does your husband feel that way in the environment of your home?

One man confessed to me that he hates being home. He and his wife have been married for over twenty years. This man loves his wife and children, but he finds any excuse to be somewhere other than in their home. "I can never do enough to make my family happy. I always feel like I'm messing up."

In this chapter, we will look at four domestic danger zones that can create conflict and represent relational turmoil in your marriage: household responsibilities, money, in-laws, and parenting. As you might imagine, each of these could be a separate chapter or even the topic of its own book. While these four areas represent unique challenges to your marriage, there are some common threads of wisdom as you approach them. Let's hit on those commonalities and then we will dive into some basic strategies on each of the danger zones.

Approaching Danger Zones

Start with Common Goals

In all the areas I mentioned, you and your husband will have different ways of approaching your life together. Let's take money for example. Your husband is ferociously saving for retirement, but you want to live a little now. You constantly argue about any extra income because he wants to save it, but you want to go on vacation or buy a new couch. It's easy to identify where you are at odds, but harmony actually starts by remembering where you agree. Bring the conversation back to the goals and values you share. These may be things like:

- ❦ We agree that we don't want to go into debt.

- ❦ We agree that we want to honor God with our money.

- We agree that both of our perspectives on money are important and we need to listen to each other.

- We agree that, if possible, we want to save x amount of money each month toward retirement.

With every aspect of your marriage, begin by affirming the larger vision of what you are working toward. You may have different approaches toward disciplining your children, but you both want to raise children who treat people with respect and have good character. Although you have different definitions of clean, you both want a home where people feel comfortable visiting. Coming back to these points of agreement will reinforce your commitment as you navigate through differences.

> With every aspect of your marriage, begin by affirming the larger vision of what you are working toward.

You and your husband may disagree on some really big issues. Finding common ground can be particularly challenging if you are married to a man who doesn't share your spiritual beliefs and commitments. The Bible describes being married to someone who doesn't share our faith like two oxen, yoked together but pulling in different directions.[i] You may relate to that feeling. Even if your husband is a Christian, you can still feel spiritually mismatched if your relationship with God is more important to you than your husband's relationship with God is to him. Maybe you want to tithe or observe the Sabbath principle by not working on Saturday or Sunday, but he doesn't agree.

God is with you if you find yourself in this situation. Both in I Peter 3:1 and in I Corinthians 7:14, God says that He can use your faith as a refining influence in your husband's life. You can still find common ground around wise living and important character qualities with a man who doesn't share your faith. The principles you've learned in this book about building into your husband as a leader can be even more powerful and profound in this situation. You may need to revisit Chapters 4, 5, 6, and 7 to tease out how to walk through disagreements and when to stand on your convictions.

There Will Always Be a Tension of Us Versus You Plus Me

I was recently talking with Dr. Greg Smalley, a well-known marriage expert. He mentioned how he cringes every time he sees a unity candle at a wedding ceremony. If you've never seen a unity candle, basically the wedding begins with two candles lit. The bride and groom each blow out their candles and together light another candle in the center. Symbolically, the candles represent that the husband and wife are no longer their own people, but together they have become one. The reason Greg doesn't like this imagery is because it suggests that your identity becomes completely forged with your spouse when you get married. You cease to be your own person.[ii]

While marriage does mean being united, you are still an individual with your own opinions, ideas, values, and preferences. You and your husband are unique people. You have your own relationship with God and your own journey toward maturity.

Think about all the stories of people in the Bible. How often are a husband and wife described as one person rather than presented in the context of their unique choices and callings? Even with married couples like Abraham and Sarah, David and Bathsheba, God speaks to them as individuals. We don't meet Peter's wife even though we know he was married. God doesn't first and foremost see you as a wife to your husband. He sees you as an individual responsible for your choices, your faith in Him, and your stewardship of what He has entrusted to you, including the stewardship of your marriage.

A healthy marriage exists with a tension of who we become as a couple while also retaining a strong sense of who we are individually.

A healthy marriage exists with a tension of who we become as a couple while also retaining a strong sense of who we are individually. Neither of you should be absorbed into the personality of the other. You are not responsible for how your husband parents, how he spends money, or how he chooses to respond to God. Understanding these boundaries will keep you in the realm of *influence* rather than trying to *control*. Your husband needs to have the freedom to do things the way he does them. The goal is not to make him a masculine version of you.

Maintaining a healthy sense of self will also remind you that you need to nurture your own relationship with the Lord. Happiness and contentment are not about achieving some perfect marriage. Being a faithful wife and having a great marriage don't always go together. Even when marriage may be crumbling, your walk with the Lord can be secure.

Balance Each Other Instead of Polarizing

One of the greatest ongoing conflicts early in my marriage was how my husband and I approached responsibility. He had a much more laid-back approach to life than I did. Mike had always had a job since he was fifteen. As a teenager, he paid for his own braces and anything else outside essentials. He learned to enjoy his time off, milking the most out of every weekend and vacation. Although he knew how to work hard, Mike loved to relax and have a good time.

I grew up very differently. I was raised by two firstborns and instilled with a sense of uber responsibility. Neither of my parents have ever been good at laughing or relaxing. One of the things that I love about Mike is that I could have fun with him. When we got married, this same trait annoyed me. Because he wanted to relax when he was home, I felt even more responsibility to stay on top of the housework, parenting, and our spiritual disciplines. The more I leaned into that responsibility, the further he shied away from it. Not long into our marriage, I started feeling resentment toward Mike. He also resented me because I was becoming like a bossy mother, always reminding him of what needed to be done.

We realized that our differences were pushing us further into our own weaknesses rather than balancing us out as people. This was happening in every area of our home life: money, house-work, parenting, and our spiritual growth. Had we continued with that pattern, not only would our marriage have suffered, but we wouldn't have grown as people. We have intentionally worked on appreciating each other and learning from each other. Over time, we have helped each other have a healthier work/play balance.

Your natural pattern will be to polarize into what feels comfort-able. If one of you dominates the conversation, the other will just stay quiet. If one of you always wins arguments, the other will never stand his ground. A healthy marriage will push into the tension of balance rather than settling for a dance that seems comfortable.

I'll repeat a theme I've hit on in earlier chapters: The dynamics you're building as a couple are more important than how you approach these domestic areas of your marriage. How neat your house is, how much savings you have in the bank, whether or not your kids eat broccoli, whose family you spend Christmas with...these things are important, but they are not as important as honoring God in how you treat each other. Be aware of how these dynamics play out in the everyday life of living together.

Household Responsibilities

Household chores represent probably the most pressing minor issue in marriage for a lot of couples because they are a conflict that never goes away. Every day, someone has to do the dishes, take out the trash, do laundry, cook dinner, and clean the sink. There's no vacation from housework. Dust doesn't stop collecting because you need a break. This means that if you have conflict about household responsibilities, it will always impact the emotional environment of your home. A romantic evening in your bedroom turns into a fight about the dirty underwear on the floor or the mold growing in the shower.

I know a couple that has a great marriage in practically every other area, but this one is enough to make my friend want to call it quits. Her husband has a lot of great qualities, but he's very messy. He grew up with a full-time mom who cooked, cleaned, and picked up his laundry off the floor. His wife wasn't aware that she was signing up for this role when they got married!

You and your husband could argue for days about chores, but ultimately it will boil down to these triggers: fairness, acceptance, and appreciation.

Fairness

Let's start with what's fair. A study found that homeowners spend an average of ninety minutes a day on housework, including household chores, maintenance, and yard work. That's over ten hours a week just to take care of your home. (If you live in an apartment, you can get away with about seven hours a week of housework.)[iii] If you add shopping, paying bills, and childcare, household responsibilities can easily represent a full-time job.

One of the mistakes young couples make is dividing up chores based on how they saw their parents do things. If Dad always paid the bills and Mom always cooked, you naturally assume that's the right way to do things. While there are some chores that have traditionally been assigned to men or women, these are really pretty arbitrary. Your parents' marriage is not your marriage. The overall responsibilities of housework, careers, and childcare may look very different.

In deciding what's fair, you need to look together at everything that needs to be done to keep your home and family functioning. There were times in my marriage when I felt like I was shouldering more of the work, but then Mike reminded me of the weekends he spent in the yard, the mornings shoveling snow, and the nights he spent paying bills and preparing taxes.

Over the seasons of our marriage, we've shifted household responsibilities depending not only on what's going on at home but also considering the demands of our respective jobs. At really busy times of work and traveling, we have paid someone to help with childcare, grooming the dogs, or cleaning. Regardless of who is doing what, the most important thing has been for us to address times when one of us felt an unfair or unsustainable burden.

Acceptance

Acceptance is also a big part of addressing conversations around chores. Chances are that one of you has a different definition of a job well done than the other. Maybe you hate the way your husband loads the dishwasher, mows the lawn, or folds clothes. He has his own way and timing of getting things done. This is one of those differences between you two that is never going to be resolved. Accept it and learn to navigate through it so you don't build up forty years of resentment over something as minor as a messy car. This means that you and your husband will have to learn to let some things go and to give each other "love gifts." There are some things I do around our house just because they matter to Mike. For example, he doesn't like to carry a big ring of keys. Instead, we keep the car keys and house key all separated. We have a place in our kitchen where everyone puts keys, so we don't lose them. If it were just me, I'd do this differently, but it's a small thing I do to accommodate Mike. He makes similar adjustments out of love for me. (Mike wants me to make sure you know how often I would lose the keys without this system. ☺)

Appreciation

You will also run into serious tension in your marriage if one or both of you feels unappreciated for what you contribute. The frustrating thing about housework is that it needs to be done over and over again. The entire house was clean for five minutes. Your refrigerator was stocked for half a day. Your kids were fed only until the next meal. The weeds were all gone for just a few days. Because your work needs to consistently be redone, it's easy to go unnoticed. And unnoticed means unappreciated.

To set a tone for appreciating the little things, you can start first. Be intentional about noticing and saying thank you when your husband empties the trash, picks up the dry cleaning, or changes the diaper. This might even start a conversation about how you're learning to say thank you for little things that you usually take for granted. Most likely, your husband will begin noticing those little things you do as well.

Money

It's More Than Dollars and Cents

At first glance, finances seem kind of boring. Budgets, bills, paychecks—they are simply a bunch of numbers. Money is so powerful, not just because of what it can buy, but because of what it represents.

> Money is so powerful, not just because of what it can buy, but because of what it represents.

Luke grew up during hard financial times. His parents had to work very hard just to meet basic expenses. Throughout his childhood, there were many things that Luke was unable to do because of financial constraints. He was one of the only sixth-graders to miss the class trip to Washington, D.C. When his friends were going on dates and playing basketball, he worked two jobs. He wore his brother's worn-out clothes that always seemed to hang from his small frame. Remembering the disappointments and embarrassments of his past, money was an important symbol of success for Luke. He wanted to drive nice cars and wear expensive clothes to show that he'd overcome his past.

Luke's wife viewed money very differently. She also grew up in a lower-middle-class home. Her father worked hard to earn a decent wage, but Selah's parents had not been careful with their money. After a few bad decisions, the family had lost their home. She remembered her parents fighting about money and wondering how they would make ends meet. To Selah, money meant safety and security. As a young teen, she learned to always be careful with her money and to spend only what was necessary.

By the time she met Luke, Selah had a good amount in her

savings. Luke noticed Selah's frugal nature and loved to spoil her with the things she would never buy for herself. By the end of their first year of marriage, money had become a major source of conflict. To Luke, having nice things meant success and respect. To Selah, it reflected recklessness.

Every time Luke made a lavish purchase, Selah interpreted his actions as not caring about her fears. When Selah brought up Luke's spending, he saw her standing in the way of his happiness. Neither of them was trying to hurt the other. They were defending their own emotional turf.

It is impossible to successfully navigate money issues in a marriage without understanding what it symbolizes for each person. Money represents very strong fears and drives. When a husband or wife ignores the emotional side to money, they can be pouring salt into an open wound. Every financial decision is also an emotional one.

> It is impossible to successfully navigate money issues in a marriage without understanding what it symbolizes for each person. . . . Every financial decision is also an emotional one.

You and your husband may want to check out resources like *The 5 Money Personalities* by Scott and Bethany Palmer to learn how to understand what money means to each of you.

Take a Team Approach

Although one person is usually responsible for actually paying the bills, both of you should be involved in your finances. There are many reasons for this. You both need to be aware of the family's financial matters in case of emergency or illness. Two different perspectives on money can help keep the family financially balanced. And both of you need to feel that your interests and concerns are considered. A team approach to finances also takes the brunt of responsibility off one person. Perhaps most importantly, it provides an aspect of accountability.

I've met with wives who are shocked to learn that their husbands have fallen thousands of dollars into debt over the years or to find out that he has burned through their savings for retirement by gambling on high-risk investments. I know husbands who are furious to discover that they cannot take out a loan because of the credit card debt their wives have secretly accumulated. All these scenarios could have been avoided with a team approach.

As a team, put together a budget. Dave Ramsey's "Financial Peace University," which you can access online at *ramseysolutions.com,* is one of the many helpful tools to do this well. Then, regularly (monthly or quarterly) review your budget, credit card statements, and general expenses.

Money problems are often due to impulsive spending that budgeting can prevent. In fact, salespeople make a living based on impulsive purchases. They are trained to encourage a consumer to buy without thinking, planning, or consulting. A couple tosses around the idea to buy a new car as their old one is becoming unreliable; they take a Saturday to visit some dealerships. They have done little research on cars, have not discussed what they can afford, and are not planning to buy a car that day. Naively, they walk into the first dealership and immediately an enthusiastic salesperson pounces on them. Within five minutes, they are test-driving a top-of-the-line model. Leather seats, all the latest tech, turbo engine. The couple begins to leave for the next dealership. Not wanting to lose the sale, the salesperson reminds them that the special rebate deal is only good for today. Within an hour, the couple has signed the papers and committed to a car that is beyond their means.

Weeks later, they realize the financial bind they are in. What seemed to be such a good decision has severely limited their financial freedom for years to come. If they had committed to a certain figure before they began their shopping or had left their checkbook at home, their problem may have been avoided.

Setting a budget together also sets the table for healthier conversations if something goes wrong. The budget becomes the bad guy. Marcy and Jim had agreed to spend $600 total on Christmas presents ($300 for each). Marcy spent her $300. Jim went a little overboard, spending more than $500 on his friends and family. Because they had agreed on $600, she could say to him, "Do you remember what we had budgeted for Christmas? I am upset that you broke the agreement we made."

Their decision had been mutually agreed upon, so their commitment, not Marcy, was the standard. Had they not talked about the budget ahead of time, this probably would have set them up for a fight.

Not only does spending or saving money tap into emotions. While they might never speak it out loud, the money a husband and wife earn can represent power in their relational dynamics. This is particularly true when it comes to budgeting. If you earn the majority of the money, you may feel like you have more say in how to spend it. If your husband has a higher paying job, you may consistently defer to him.

A team approach will never think about money this way. My dad earned all the money in our family, but my mom ran a house with six children. She cooked, hosted Bible studies at our house several times a week, was my dad's greatest advisor, and managed all our doctor appointments and activities. While she was never paid for her contributions, she worked as hard (if not harder) than my dad. What my dad earned, they earned together.

Have Both Transparency and Freedom

Part of the unity of marriage is sharing money, but it is also important for both the husband and wife to have some of their own money. I'm not suggesting having secret bank accounts or credit lines. Everything you do financially should be transparent. However, it's also often helpful for both you and your husband to have some financial freedom (consistent with what you can afford) to spend or save the way each of you'd like to.

Even if you can only budget a small amount a month as discretionary personal spending, having some financial freedom can be a release valve for your marriage.

Maybe you want to be able to go out to lunch with friends without feeling guilty about it or you like expensive coffee drinks as a treat. Maybe one of you is a big gift giver and doesn't feel the freedom to express love this way. Having your own discretionary money can help alleviate a lot of arguments and resentment. Even if you can only budget a small amount a month as discretionary personal spending, having some financial freedom can be a release valve for your marriage.

In-Laws

There is a reason why the Bible describes marriage as a combination of "leaving and cleaving." You can't fully cleave until you both have done the leaving. If you want to get a group of guys to talk, just bring up the topic of mothers-in-law. And it's not like women don't have their own mothers-in-law stories! While the classic mother-in-law battle represents a lot of marriages, this is not the only way that family dynamics can create havoc for your marriage (and not all mothers-in-law are bad!). Your and your husband's families, whether you are close to them or not, have had a great deal of influence on how you view relationships, conflict, male and female, sex, money, and pretty much every aspect of marriage. You are wise to be mindful of this influence.

Don't Live in the Shadows of Greatness or Failure

Even as adults, we are prone to view our parents as either better or worse than they actually are. This is because of something psychologists call splitting. As a young child, you can only see people and experiences as either all good or all bad. This explains why children's cartoons and stories have heroes and villains. Making sense of the world means that my family is all good and the rest of the world is dangerous. Or, Mom is good and Dad is bad. Or, my parents are good and I'm bad. As we grow, we develop the capacity to live with the complexity of human motives and behavior. No one is all good, nor is anyone all bad. People are an intricate mix of virtue and vice.

Because our family relationships were forged in childhood, sometimes we still apply these good and bad categories to parents and siblings, even after we have grown to have more nuanced relationships elsewhere. Being around your mom or dad can emotionally transport you to that little girl who feels ashamed or terrified of losing a parent's approval.

Most people come into a marriage with an unconscious motivation to either repeat what they grew up with (my family is all good) or to rebel against it (my family is all bad). Have you ever had the thought, *Oh my goodness, I'm becoming my mom!*? Or maybe you secretly wished your husband were more like your dad.

On the one hand, be grateful for what's good about your parents, but don't fall into the trap of thinking they did everything the best way. On the other hand, be aware of their weaknesses but don't live in fear of repeating them. You and your husband are forging your own traditions, your own style of relating, and walking your unique journey as husband and wife.

Your parents and in-laws can be great encouragers in your marriage, but they can also be saboteurs. While they want you to be happy, they may also believe that happiness means staying emotionally close to them. Here's an example.

Your parents and in-laws can be great encouragers in your marriage, but they can also be saboteurs.

Rene deeply loved her family and had a great relationship with her dad. He was hard-working, sensitive, and attentive. He would give anything for his little girl. Even through the awkwardness of adolescence, Rene's dad was her hero.

When Rene fell in love with Brad, her dad was happy for her. With tears in his eyes and a lump in his throat, he walked Rene down the aisle to her new life. He was so proud of her. He believed she could do anything. He liked Brad but secretly worried that this young man was too immature to take care of his little girl.

Rene and Brad rented an apartment ten minutes away from her family. The couple experienced the normal stress and conflict of newlyweds and at times their conflicts became heated. Brad turned stone silent when he was angry. Rene could not understand why he clammed up in the middle of an argument.

When she felt discouraged, Rene would sometimes jump into her beat-up car and drive to the safety and comfort of her childhood home. She and her dad would have tea and talk about her dilemma. Her father always wanted to help. Throughout their marriage, Rene's father offered financial assistance, job references for Brad, good advice, and a shoulder to cry on.

Although Brad appreciated the intentions of his father-in-law, something inside him also resented this man. Brad felt like a child still trying to court his wife. He believed he would never be good enough, old enough, stable enough, or rich enough to take care of her. Brad knew that Rene admired her father more than she admired anyone else.

You might feel this same way about your mother-in-law. She still wants to be the most important woman in your husband's life. You're constantly aware of the tension of who he will choose... you or his mom. Your mother-in-law may be a wonderful woman, but there is always an unspoken feeling that you're not good enough for her son.

A good family is truly a blessing from God, but the relationship between a parent and child must change with time. Your parents will always be your parents, but you can't live in the shadow of their help or the pressure to please them. This leaving doesn't happen when you drive off to your honeymoon. It may take years to establish your own identity as a couple.

Set Boundaries with Grace

Navigating relationships with parents means one very important thing: setting boundaries. Most well-meaning parents are not aware of the ways they may manipulate or otherwise put pressure on your marriage. Other parents seem oblivious to the damage they do by their demands, rude criticism, and threats.

For almost every couple, "leaving" mother and father means intentionally making decisions that indicate, "We are our own family now." Henry Cloud and John

For almost every couple, "leaving" mother and father means intentionally making decisions that indicate, "We are our own family now."

Townsend have written a great series of books about boundaries that can be helpful in doing this well. In general, it is better for you and your husband to discuss boundaries with your *own parents* rather than having conversations with your in-laws. You have the emotional equity with your parents, and your husband has it with his. These boundaries might include things like spending every other Christmas with each family, setting limits for financial help so you don't feel the strings often attached to money, not sharing marriage problems with parents, and having rules like "don't stop over unless you call first." You might have to address more subtle boundary violations.

Amber and Jeremy have two young daughters. Jeremy's mom loves being a grandmother and often offers to watch the girls. This is a great help, but whenever the girls stay over at "Mimi's" house, they are hyper from sugar and crabby because they don't take a nap. Mimi tells Amber, "Spoiling them is part of being a grand-mother!" While this is true, it's also important that Mimi respects how Amber and Jeremy are parenting. Jeremy needs to have a loving and firm talk with his mom that may go something like this:

> *Thank you so much for watching the girls. They love being with you, and it's a real gift to Amber and me. We'd love for you to continue to watch them whenever you'd like to. There is one issue I need to talk to you about. We have a set of rules at our house about what the girls eat, when they go to bed, and so on, . . . you have a different set of rules when they are over here. That's fine if they are visiting for an hour, but when they are here for a while, it throws everything off for us once we get them home. (Maybe share an example.) I need to ask you to follow some basic guidelines when you have the girls so they can continue to spend time with you.*

Usually, if you set and reinforce solid boundaries early in your marriage, you can relax them over time. While it might seem harsh to set boundaries with the mom or dad who raised you, you can do so with grace. It's right to have empathy for how difficult it is for your parents or in-laws to let go. While children are told to obey their parents, adult children are commanded to honor their parents. Even while setting boundaries, treat them with honor and dignity. It deeply saddens me when I hear stories of adult children who refuse to see their parents or withhold grandchildren. Yes, there are extreme examples of abuse that require separation, but you can extend grace and mercy by sending cards and finding ways to love even with distance.

Parenting

"I am having a baby!" These five words change your life forever. It doesn't take long for your body to begin forcing that change. Before you know it, every older woman you know starts giving you advice on pregnancy, breastfeeding, and every other aspect of motherhood.

Your husband's metamorphosis is probably slower. There are no showers for him at work or helpful advice from veterans...just awkward jokes about how "my boys can swim." Parenting is a long journey. Variables like stepchildren, raising children with developmental delays, or attachment injuries make the parenting journey even more complicated. If you are not a united team, your marriage may not survive the stress of parenting. While every family is different, here are some basic principles that can help you navigate parenthood together.

Keep Your Marriage Central

The love a mother has for her child is perhaps the strongest emotion that a person experiences. Although it is a different kind of love, many women confess that they feel more bonded with their children than with their husbands. It's normal for a mom to be obsessed with her baby in the first few months (remember what you learned about oxytocin?). There are other seasons (like a child with a serious illness or the early years of blending a new family) where your energy and resources have to focus on the children. But if the priority of your marriage isn't reestablished, you can fall into the trap of depending upon your children to meet your emotional needs. This is harmful not only for your marriage but also for your children's development.

When the kids were younger, Mike sometimes told me that he felt like he was always getting "the leftovers." Even when we were alone, I was prone to run to the boys as soon I heard a whimper out of one of them. I couldn't relax when I was away from them because I was afraid something would happen. I had to force myself to regularly schedule date nights and occasional weekend getaways. I wanted to spend time with my husband, but my kids' needs were so much more obvious. I had to remind myself often that one of the best gifts I could give my children was growing up in a home with a solid marriage.

We are now entering the empty nest. I'm so thankful that Mike reminded me to keep building our marriage through the busy years of raising kids! We are actually looking forward to this new season, because we invested in each other while working up to it.

Give Him the Gift of Your Children's Love

Counselors sometimes refer to the mother as the "translator." Moms constantly find themselves interpreting and communicating between fathers and their children. A teen's mother will explain his father's curt response to the boy's request to use the car. "Your dad had a bad day. I'll talk to him about it when he calms down."

Think about the power of being a translator between your husband and your children. You get to determine how your children see and understand their father.

"Mommy, where is Daddy? Why can't he play with me?" Most moms respond to this kind of question without even a second thought. How she responds over time to these questions will impact this girl's view of her daddy. A neutral response may be, "He's at work, Honey." If she is angry at her husband, she might say, "Daddy isn't home a lot. He's usually out doing his own thing." A thoughtful wife can frame her answer in a way that builds up her husband by saying, "I know Daddy would love to play with you, but he goes to work so we can have food, a home, and clothes to wear. Maybe we can plan to have a tea party with him tonight."

Think about the differences between those three responses. All three of them probably reflect the truth. Dad has both altruistic and selfish reasons for working hard. The ones that are reinforced by his wife will become the reasons his child remembers. This is not only true about what a wife says about work but about every aspect of Dad. How he disciplines, why he is quiet sometimes, and how he spends money.

One woman shared a memory that symbolized the love with which her mother spoke of her father. One year, her father gave her mother a harp for Christmas. When she opened the gift, the mother exclaimed to the kids, "Do you know how many hours your father worked to buy me this harp? This is the most precious gift I have ever received!" Even as an adult, that woman remembers a picture of a loving, generous father. A mother can teach her children to hate a loving father or to love a father who often failed.

> A mother can teach her children to hate a loving father or to love a father who often failed.

I learned this principle from my mom. She had a huge role in forging the beautiful relationship I have with my father. As a self-employed businessman, my dad traveled often. During my childhood, he was gone a lot. My mom was never critical of him. I remember my time with Dad as special. As an adult, my dad told me, "I must be the happiest man on the face of the Earth. Do you know why I am so happy?" he asked me. "Because all six of my children love me. Your mother gave me that gift."

Help Him to Be a Good Dad

When I became a mother, I was amazed at how often women compare mothering notes. Bible studies, at the park, at the grocery store—everywhere I went; I felt I was in a giant support group of moms who were all experiencing similar stresses. Over time, I naturally became an expert on caring for my children. My husband didn't have this advantage. He had no idea that raisins cause diarrhea, that teething babies drool, that kids get hyperactive when they are tired, or that teens can't tell you when they are sad. Parenting blogs and the ability to google common questions have helped dads feel more prepared, but this information is still more commonly shared among women. This puts dads at a disadvantage.

Imagine a well-meaning father playing with his five-month-old baby. He jiggles her, shakes her, and throws her in the air. Mom sees their playtime and remembers the dangers of shaking a baby. She immediately corrects him. So, the dad moves on to his seven-year-old son. They are playing catch with a football. The boy drops the ball and the father playfully responds, "Come on, Butterfingers!" Mom has recently read that negative words can hurt the boy's self-esteem, so she tells her husband not to call him names like that. He looks at his twelve-year-old daughter and thinks, *I'm not even going to try to figure out that one!*

Here is the dilemma for every mother: How do you help your husband succeed as a parent without discouraging him with your criticism or humiliating him with constant advice? Here are three simple steps that can go a long way in achieving this goal.

1. LET SOME THINGS GO.

There are many things in parenting that can be critical to a child's safety and development, but there are other things that are just not that important. So, the kid's outfit doesn't match or they got to bed an hour late. When you are bothered by something your husband is doing with the children, ask yourself how important it is in the long run. If it is not a big deal, ignore it. Sometimes, dads are just being dads, not moms. When our kids were little, I saw counseling clients two evenings a week. Mike and I would high-five as he came home and I left for work, passing the parenting baton. Usually, I had dinner made for Mike and the boys. I can't tell you how many nights I got home from work and realized that he had ordered pizza and watched a Disney movie with the boys. I spent all day trying to help them eat healthy and avoid screen time and then Disney Dad swoops in for the fun! I learned that sometimes I just had to let it go (no pun intended if you're a *Frozen* fan). This was how Mike had fun with the kids when he was tired at the end of a workday.

2. ENCOURAGE HIM.

All of us respond so much better to positive feedback than criticism. If you're honest as a mom, you'll admit to often feeling inadequate. It's impossible to always know exactly what to do. You lose your temper; you let the kids have too much screen time; you don't know how to make the baby stop crying or how to get your teenager to listen. Whenever I am with an encouraging friend, I feel refreshed. "Juli, you're a great mom. You're so intentional about teaching your boys how to interact with others." These encouragements have often kept me going through the parenting journey. I want to give my husband the same encouragement and grace that I know I need.

3. MAKE SOMEONE ELSE THE EXPERT.

As a mom, you have important information that can be very helpful to your husband as a father. He is much more likely to accept that information if it does not come directly from you. I'm saying this even as a clinical psychologist. Although I've learned how to be a pretty good mom, I don't know how to be a good dad. My husband needs someone other than me to be his coach or critic! Find resources so that you can learn together. Read books, attend parenting classes at church, listen to a podcast, or meet with a mentor couple.

The Grace Zone

It's interesting to write this chapter after twenty-seven years of marriage. Lord willing, Mike and I have many years ahead of us, but we also have a lot of years behind us. In each of these categories, we've made some mistakes. Some of our bad decisions were not significant, but others were. Just yesterday we were talking about what we would do differently if we could raise our kids all over again. We have some regrets. "But we still have today," we remind each other.

Friend, you are not going to do this perfectly and neither is your husband. No one does. You'll make mistakes with your money, family relationships, friendships, and parenting. Your weaknesses and immaturity will at times get the best of you. But here's the deal . . . you don't really know how amazing grace is until you need it.

Christianity is a relationship with God built on receiving His grace for you. He forgives your sin. He covers your failings. He gives you strength in your weakness, courage in your fear, and wisdom in your foolishness.

Making home a restful place is truly only possible if you are walking in this grace of God because you cannot give a grace that you have not first received. You can love and invest in your husband because you know a God who loves and invests in you.

Endnotes

i   2 Corinthians 6:4.

ii We discuss this on Java with Juli #327, "When your spouse feels more like a roommate," August 2020.

iii https://www.cnbc.com/2018/09/21/apartment-list-time-owners-spend-on -housework-compared-to-renters.html#:~:text=They%20found%20that% 20on%20average,week%2C%20or%20over%2010%20hours.

Chapter 11

work: his, mine, and ours

There are some aspects of the Christian life that most of us think don't matter too much to God. Unless you or your husband are in full-time ministry, you might think of work as one of those categories.

One of the devil's most effective strategies is convincing Christians to live divided or compartmentalized lives. We think about God when we have our devotions, when we go to church, and when we need help. But the Christian life God calls you to is 100 percent an integrated life.

The most important commandment in the Bible is this one: Love the Lord your God with *all* your heart and with *all* your soul and with *all* your mind. The second most important commandment is the overflow of this love for God in our relationships: "Love your neighbor as yourself." Jesus said that everything God wants you to do can be summed up in those two commandments.[i]

Work is not a category of your life or your marriage. It is the overflow of your personhood. As I've grown in my relationship with the Lord, there are many things He has taught me about work that have impacted how I approach both my work and my husband's.

First of all, work is not just what we get paid to do. When Jesus talked to a Samaritan woman at a well (see John 4), He was taking a break from traveling. Yet, He described this conversation as His work and doing the work of the Father. As a woman, it's always kind of awkward to know how to ask other women about work. I've been asked, "Do you work?" Of course I work, even if that work isn't classified as a career or a job. Your work is not just your vocation but can include community involvement, taking care of your children and home, and serving at church.

I've also learned that what I do is far less important to God than how I do it. In Colossians 3, Paul addressed slaves whose work was redundant, despised, and trivial. He elevated the purpose of their work by reminding them, "Whatever you do, work at it with all your heart, as working for the Lord, not for human masters, *since* you know that you will receive an inheritance from the Lord as a reward. It is the Lord Christ you are serving."[ii]

Some work is more spiritual than other work, not because of what you may be doing, but because of the heart from which you are doing it. I've done ministry work from a selfish, proud heart, and I've done secular and menial work with a servant heart. I have no doubt that the latter was more glorifying to God than the former.

> Some work is more spiritual than other work, not because of what you may be doing, but because of the heart from which you are doing it.

Think of work like a car. While there are some cars that are faster, fancier, and more fun to drive than others, the primary purpose of a car is transportation. Throughout your lifetime, you've probably ridden in and owned many cars. Each was for a season.

If you loved the car too much, you missed the point of owning it. A car is a temporary means to an end. What really matters is whether the car is functional, how you drive it, and where it takes you. The same is true of your work. You and your husband will have many different jobs, some paid and others unpaid. What matters is not the title, salary, or prestige of each job, but the heart from which you serve.

Both you and your husband have been given a commission during your time on Earth. Your work has threads of one commission in Genesis, "Be fruitful and multiply and have dominion over the earth,"[iii] and Jesus's expansion of that to His disciples, "Go into all the world and preach the gospel, teaching people to obey what I have said."[iv] One commission addresses how we steward the physical earth and the other has to do with investing in the eternal kingdom. God has also given you and your husband talents (time, natural abilities, spiritual gifts, energy) to invest in order to accomplish your commission. The various jobs, tasks, relationships, material possessions, and careers you have are the vehicles through which you walk out God's will for you. This will be true whether you are serving your neighbor, making a million dollars, or working in a dead-end job.

In many parts of the world, work is simply survival. Only recently and within wealthy countries do we have the luxury to think about what we'd like to do with our lives and how our work can best express our longings and giftedness. It is definitely a blessing for both you and your husband to be able to choose a career, but that freedom can also create frustration and tension. In his book *Just Do Something*, Kevin DeYoung tackles the paralysis and anxiety a lot of young adults feel facing the endless choices of marriage, careers, and callings. "Go get a job, provided it's not wicked...But put aside the passivity and the quest for complete fulfillment and the perfectionism and the preoccupation with the future, and for God's sake start making some decisions in your life. Don't wait for the liver shiver. If you are seeking first the kingdom of God and His righteousness, you will be in God's will, so just go out and do something."[v]

Most of us spend a lot of time obsessing about what car we will be driving instead of focusing on where that car is taking us. Whether you are a teacher, a doctor, an artist, a mom, or an Uber driver, the question is "How do I use this present 'car' to do the eternal work that really matters?" As with any other area of life, God cares about your heart a lot more than your accomplishments.

Now let's apply this principle to the realities of navigating careers.

Understanding Your Husband's Work

I was a young therapist when Bob, a man in his mid-fifties, scheduled an appointment to meet with me. Bob had recently been laid off from his job as a medical sales rep. Week after week, he came in for counseling to talk about his depression and feelings of failure and worthlessness. Of course, I never told Bob this, but as an optimistic (and naive) young woman, I couldn't understand why getting laid off was such a big deal to this man. I wanted to say, "Okay, so you lost your job. Go find a new one." But Bob was so discouraged, he couldn't find the energy to apply and interview for a new job. I also didn't understand the complexity and fear of applying for a job as a fifty-five-year-old.

Work ups and downs affect both men and women. It would feel awful to get fired, laid off, or be underemployed. I didn't then understand that while men and women are impacted by work, they are not always impacted the same way. My hunch is that if Bob were "Roberta," we may have had a very different conversation processing the loss of a job. While work is important to both men and women, it often carries a weightier significance in a man's life.

Why Work Matters to Your Husband

The next time you and your husband meet some new friends, pay attention to how long it takes before one of the guys begins talking about work. It's one of the first questions a guy gets asked when he meets another man. "What line of work are you in?" Culturally, women have more acceptable options. You can work full-time, part-time, volunteer in the community, school, or church, or be a stay-at-home mom. Some couples are breaking this mold with more options for guys to have work flexibility or stay at home. The COVID-19 pandemic has led to even more potential flexibility in hours and work environments. Even so, work is a central aspect of a man's identity. And I don't think this is just culturally driven.

The Bible doesn't clearly say, "Men work, and women stay home." Both men and women should be diligent and work hard. God told both Adam and Eve, "Be fruitful and multiply. Subdue the earth." A man and woman share in the responsibility for family life and impacting the greater world. Even so, there are clues in the Bible indicating a man's primary bend toward work and a woman's greater focus on relationships.

In Genesis 3, God told Adam and Eve the impact of their sin on their lives and offspring. Notice the difference in focus to the man and the woman.

To Eve, He said, "I will surely multiply your pain in childbearing; in pain you shall bring forth children. Your desire shall be for your husband, and he shall rule over you."

To Adam, He said, "Because you have listened to the voice of your wife and have eaten of the tree of which I commanded you, 'You shall not eat of it,' cursed is the ground because of you; in pain you shall eat of it all the days of your life; thorns and thistles it shall bring forth for you; and you shall eat the plants of the field. By the sweat of your face, you shall eat bread, till you return to the ground..."

> While there is no cut-and-dried command about gender and work in the Bible, there is a pattern suggesting that work has a different significance for men that transcends culture.

Why do you think in the very beginning, the focus of a man and woman's joy and frustration would be so different? While there is no cut-and-dried command about gender and work in the Bible, there is a pattern suggesting that work has a different significance for men that transcends culture.

In the early chapters of this book, we explored how key the issue of competence is in your husband's life. The central drama for most men is this question: Will I be known as a capable, dependable person who makes a mark on this world? For many men, the center stage of that drama involves his career, his dreams, and his work.

Your husband's work is not just what he does to bring in money. It likely represents why he feels valuable to you and to the world in general. While some men attack the challenge of work with confidence and drive, others retreat into passivity because they fear failure.

Interestingly, many last names have been derived from the work that ancestors once performed. Years ago, it was Jim the blacksmith, Sam the baker, Tom the cook, and George the fisher. In truth, men are still identified by what they do. It often defines them in the world's eyes. A man's survival and social standing often seem to depend on their work status. Even while performing a worthwhile task that provides a healthy income, a man can feel like a failure next to someone who has more prestige or earns more money.

Bob didn't come to counseling because he lost his job. He came to see me because he felt like he had lost his identity. Bob didn't hear his boss say, "We hate to lose you, but the company is facing some financially tough times." Instead, he heard, "Out of all the people in this company, I chose to let you go. You're not good enough." While his wife was supportive, Bob couldn't express the level of humiliation he felt at being unemployed.

Why Work Frustrates Your Husband

Work is the ultimate enigma for a man. Even if he wins the lottery and never has to do a day's work in his life, he still needs work to survive. Men who retire without replacing their paid jobs with other meaningful work often feel depressed and anxious.[vi] We see in Genesis that work is both a blessing and a curse. In the perfect world of Eden, God gave Adam a job. Work was part of his pre-fall state, but work also became a central aspect of how he would experience the brokenness of this fallen world. Even if your husband is successful, he can't escape the headaches and ultimate futility of work. Solomon, a guy who had it all, explains why.

In the book of Ecclesiastes, Solomon plays the philosopher, reflecting on his own search for meaning through his various pursuits. He starts the book of Ecclesiastes by telling you right up front his conclusion: "Meaningless! Meaningless! Utterly meaningless! Everything is meaningless! What do people gain from all their labors at which they toil under the sun?"

Solomon had wealth, power, success, pleasure, and the opportunity to impact the world, and this was his depressing conclusion. You can never earn enough money to be happy. No matter how hard you try, no one will remember you when you die. You can't invent anything that someone before you hasn't discovered. The more you learn, the more discouraged you'll become. You can't take your money or success with you when you die. Some fool will squander what you worked to acquire. No matter how altruistic you are, there will always be sick people you can't help and injustices you can't make right.

While Ecclesiastes is a bit melodramatic, it can help you understand why work is such a thorn in your husband's side. If he's successful, he's driven to make just one more deal. Constantly comparing himself to others, he can't relax. If he's just earning a paycheck at work, he feels unfilled, underemployed, bored, or unappreciated. Even if he's landed his dream job, he worries about how people perceive him and whether or not he will leave a lasting legacy.

The reason that Solomon became so depressed when he reflected on his life is because he used the vehicle of work for temporary things. Throughout Ecclesiastes, he writes about the emptiness of pleasure, power, money, and even trying to fix things here on Earth.

Solomon lived before Jesus gave us an eternal perspective. Solomon admits this when he writes,

> *What does the worker gain from his toil? I have seen the burden that God has laid upon the sons of men to occupy them. He has made everything beautiful in its time. He has also set eternity in the hearts of men, yet they cannot fathom the work that God has done from beginning to end....I*

*saw every work of God, and that a man is unable to com-
prehend the work that is done under the sun. Despite his
efforts to search it out, he cannot find its meaning; even if
the wise man claims to know, he is unable to comprehend.*

Solomon could see nothing lasting or eternal about his life, so it was ultimately meaningless. Jesus came to pull back the veil so that we can now see eternal value in potentially everything we do. Every day at work presents an opportunity to interact with people who have eternal souls. All work has the potential to be eternally meaningful.

Work is a wonderful gift, but it is a gift with thorns. The frustrations of work are part of the fall, but they are also a needed reminder for you and your husband not to invest life in things that ultimately don't matter. Praise God that work is often frustrating and unfulfilling or we would find ourselves living for a career, status, and accomplishments. "For whoever wants to save his life will lose it, but whoever loses his life for My sake and for the gospel will save it. What does it profit a man to gain the whole world, yet forfeit his soul?"[vii]

Understanding and living out this larger vision of work, like everything else in the Christian life, is a journey. As a wife, you and your husband are on this journey together.

While you probably don't work alongside your husband, you are doing life with him, which means you are intimately connected with his work journey. You see his moods impacted by the ups and downs. He might process with you the good days and bad ones. You may even get tired of hearing him talk over and over about how frustrating his job is or how much he dislikes his boss. If your husband is a driven guy, you likely see work as a competitor. When he's home, you want him to be with you, not talk about work.

You have the opportunity to intimately share one of the most important areas of your husband's life. Through his work, you can see strengths, dreams, passions, and fears that might be hidden in other areas of your marriage.

It's not your job to tell your husband how he should approach his work, but like every other area of marriage, you can influence his perspective throughout the journey. Here are a few ways to do this well.

Remind Him That His Worth Is Not His Paycheck.

Everyone cheers for a winner. It is easy for parents and friends to pay more attention to someone when they are excelling. Very few people in your husband's life will look at the man behind the career. When you are proud of him, emphasize character rather than performance: "I'm so impressed by the way you kept your cool in that situation." "You always go out of your way to encourage people. I love that about you." When he experiences setbacks and failures, focus on the man he is becoming through testing: "I know you've had a rough season at work. I just want you to know that I'm proud of you for not giving up." "You're still the same guy you were last month when you hit your sales goals. I love and respect you just as much as I did then. I'm in this with you during the good times and bad."

When a man believes his worth is linked to his title or paycheck, he may pursue work with an unhealthy perspective. Yes, men can become addicted to their jobs. Clearly it is not their work to which they are addicted—it is the excitement, the risk, the drive for success, or the fear of failure.

Be careful to encourage your husband's passion and calling, not his drive. A calling is defined by enthusiasm for something.

When a man connects with a vision or calling, he is moving toward something—a goal, a purpose, a worthy personality characteristic. When a man is driven, he is moving away from something he fears—failure, rejection, and emptiness. Callings move a person closer to their uniqueness and God-given passions. Drives move them further into the recesses of their defensiveness. A drive is characterized by compulsion that can never be fully fulfilled. Some men withdraw from work because of fear and other men become enslaved by it.

> Callings move a person closer to their uniqueness and God-given passions. Drives move them further into the recesses of their defensiveness.

Jada never worried about Lance having an affair. She knew that he loved her and that other women did not tempt him, but Jada still felt like a rejected wife. Night after night, she sat home waiting for him to come home for dinner. She looked forward to weekends when she might spend time with him. Lance was consistent. He was always working. Even on vacation, his mind was preoccupied with ideas, problems, and plans for his company. Jada felt as if her husband had a mistress—his job.

Lance worked so hard because he was driven to be the best. When everyone cleared the office at six, he stayed until nine. Naturally, he climbed the ladder of success rapidly. After years of eating, sleeping, and drinking his work, Lance had no hobbies, little time for people and no leisure. To Jada, Lance had become a working machine. Their marriage revolved around his work. He did not know how to talk about anything else. As a dutiful husband, he listened to Jada drone on about her day but with little interest. Only a distant memory was the passion they had shared while dating, when they had talked about ideas, served in a church, and dreamed of the future.

You may be the only person who knows your husband well enough to differentiate between his passion and his drive. You are likely the only one who can prompt him to think about why he works so many hours. Through your influence, you can help him address his fear and ignite his passion.

There are times, like birthdays and the New Year, when people naturally sit back and take stock of their lives. Others think about their lives while on vacation, when they have a setback or even when they are sick. Take advantage of these times when your husband is reevaluating. Help him ask the right questions. Through your thoughtful comments and prompts, ask him what he might regret years from now. Encourage him to think about why work has such a hold on him. Remind him of how important he is to you and his children. Ultimately, this is something your husband will have to address with God, but you can be an influence in asking the right questions and emphasizing your love apart from accomplishment.

Remember, It's His Job.

"I care about my husband's work. I ask him about it all the time, but he never takes my advice. He never wants to talk about his work." As damaging as it is for a wife to undervalue her husband's work, it is equally destructive for her to take personal responsibility for his job.

As a husband shares frustrations at work, some wives have a special knack for pointing out what he did wrong and how he can fix it. Mike has sometimes caught me playing the expert at his job. I was confidently giving him tips on making client calls when he reminded me of the fact that I break out in hives whenever I have to place an unpleasant call. "You have no idea what I do at work." He was right. He needed me to listen. He definitely did not need me to tell him how to do his job.

This is a tempting trap for a woman to fall into because you rely on his income as much as he does. You might feel like a helpless cheerleader on the sideline. He handles work so differently than you would. Your husband will make some mistakes. Those are his mistakes to make. Be his advocate, his friend, his encourager, and his sounding board, but don't be his boss or his critic. Rather than coaching him through his job, encourage your husband to find a mentor who knows about his job and the unique pressures of being a man.

Don't Become His Competitor.

There is nothing wrong with a woman earning more than her husband or a guy managing parenting responsibilities, but couples in this situation need to be intentional about making sure they are not working against their underlying emotional needs. It's not about who earns more money or has the prestigious job. It's about what all that represents to the couple. Remember, a man's needs are respect and companionship. A wife needs to feel valued and protected. Sometimes, career choices set a couple up for isolation in marriage because they work against their emotional needs.

Megan had a great job at an advertising firm. She earned a comfortable salary with benefits and paid vacation time. Her husband, Russ, earned less than she did. He never really liked work. He'd tried carpentry, plumbing, trucking, and sales. About a year into each job, he gave up, frustrated by the long hours and low pay.

Megan and Russ had two children within eighteen months. After brief maternity leaves, Megan returned to work and put the children in day care. The family simply could not afford to have her quit work. Not long after their second child was born, Russ again quit his job. After months of searching and interviewing, Russ decided that it would be more cost effective for him to stay home with the kids than work. As the children grew and entered school, Russ still resisted finding a job. Now thirty-five, with no college degree and no marketable skills, Russ felt useless. Why would he get a minimum-wage job while Megan's career is thriving?

The issue with Russ and Megan isn't about who stays home and who earns the paycheck but about sliding into a pattern that undercuts their emotional needs. There are plenty of situations in which a woman has the higher paying job, but the couple has dealt with issues of value, respect, and protection so that they don't end up resenting each other.

For example, I have a friend who has a high-paying, stable, and respected career. When I asked her about her career journey, she shared with me that she has always been in a steady, corporate job. Her husband is a pastor of an inner-city church serving mostly the homeless, earning little to no income. Over the years, they decided to share the household responsibilities and for my friend to be the primary wage earner. Even though the family relies on her for benefits and a paycheck, my friend deeply respects her husband's work.

This is very different from Russ and Megan, who slid into an arrangement that has ended up being a very destructive dynamic in their marriage. Megan assumed more and more power by bringing in the money and earning respect at work. Russ began hating being around her. He knew she didn't respect him because he'd lost all his self-respect. Megan loves her job but also feels resentful that she has to do the heavy lifting of providing for their family and shouldering many of the parenting responsibilities. She is often angry about having to miss out on her daughter's school performances because of work pressure.

This couple is stuck in a cycle that reinforces anger and self-protection, which is largely rooted in their respective approaches to work. For their marriage to survive, Russ needs to face his fear of failure and take meaningful steps to get to work, whatever that might look like. It doesn't matter how much or little a job might initially pay, the issue is Russ's character and confidence as a man. Megan also has a part to play in this. She can impact the dance of their marriage by changing her own approach to work. For example, Megan might cut back on her hours to force a healthier balance of responsibility between her and Russ. I'm not suggesting that Russ's career is more important than Megan's, but that their marriage is.

I have female friends who are doctors and CEOs. I also have friends who are homemakers. The health of the marriage is not about their career or paycheck but how each one has navigated the emotional issues that work represents in marriage.

The health of the marriage is not about their career or paycheck but how each one has navigated the emotional issues that work represents in marriage.

Your Work and Your Man

A few years ago, I sat down at a coffee shop with a new friend. Christine had just gotten engaged to Will, a friend who is like a brother to me. Within an hour of meeting his fiancé, I knew Will had found a treasure, but Christine had a dilemma in marrying Will. With tears in her eyes, this young woman explained to me her call to serve God in Africa.

Christine had just finished her training as an occupational therapist and was preparing for life in missions. At a global missions conference, she met Will. Although he is also passionate about missions, Will builds online platforms to support missions organizations. Christine explained her dilemma:

One month into our dating we had the hard conversation. While we both felt a strong call to serve in missions, I felt called to go and he felt called to send. It would have been easy to have rolled my eyes and said, "I'm pretty sure you're just not hearing the Lord correctly," but it was undeniable. God had equipped this man with priceless skill sets and was using him to connect thousands of individuals to opportunities to serve in missions. God was using him to have a remarkable kingdom impact.

My heart was crushed. I wanted to be this man's wife. I wanted to live a life in partnership with him, learning from him, loving him. But more deeply I wanted to be obedient to the Lord and the call He had placed on my life. I was angry, confused, and deeply saddened. Why would the Lord bring this amazing man into my life when He had called us to two different continents?

While your situation might not be exactly like Christine's, chances are you can relate to the tension of incompatible dreams, callings, and careers between you and your husband. Do you move to a new city for his job even if it disrupts yours? Will one of you work to support the other one's education? Who stays home with young children? Should you stay in a job you don't love so your husband can pursue his dream?

Recognize the Seasons

One of the keys to navigating career decisions is remembering that your life represents different seasons. This is particularly true as women. There are windows of time represented by energy, passion, fertility, and the needs of young children in the early years of marriage. Later in life, you have more wisdom, experience, and likely fewer family demands. Saying no to career opportunities for one season doesn't mean saying no forever.

I am blessed to have been raised in a home in which my parents told me I could do anything I put my mind to. They helped me figure out my gifts and supported me through my education. But I also have a wise mother who would occasionally remind me, "You can do anything, but you can't do everything. Every time you say *yes* to something, remember that you are saying *no* to something else."

I literally finished my last final for my doctorate degree the same week I gave birth to our first son. This wasn't planned. After finishing my coursework, I would have to complete a yearlong predoctoral internship. I had worked and studied for years to become a psychologist. While I wanted to be a mom, how could I do both of these things well?

Mike had worked in private banking and had just finished his MBA when we had our son. Just twenty months later, we had boy number two. Mike and I were swamped with babies, career choices, and financial pressures. He had just gotten a job at an insurance company, and we were trying to figure out who would stay home with our boys.

I realized that this was a rare season to invest in my boys and in my marriage. We decided that I would stay home with the boys, counseling a few nights a week to work toward my license. Mike would have the steady career with health benefits. In a sense, we were both sacrificing for each other. As a Marine who used to jump out of airplanes and had a pilot's license, Mike never saw himself in a corporate nine-to-five career. And I was chomping at the bit to use my freshly minted doctorate degree. We both had to trust that this was the right decision for this season and that there may be other seasons for both me and Mike to make different choices.

I also had to realize that I wasn't wasting my gifts even if I wasn't using them much professionally. What I learned in my training helped me as I was parenting, interacting with my friends and husband, and serving in my local church. Ironically, I wrote the first version of this book during that season.

I've worn a lot of hats in five decades: wife, daughter, mom, sister, author, psychologist, board member, ministry leader, speaker, and friend, but it has taken me many years to figure out which one to put on when. I would never tell another woman to follow the exact road I did. Each woman's situation and journey is unique. But I would encourage you to be mindful of each unique season of your life. What has God specifically given you to do in this season?

Trusting God with Your Dreams

Obeying God in each season will likely mean sacrificing some of your career longings. We live in a culture that has Christianized the self-help message to believe in yourself and pursue your dreams. You may have even been taught that God wants you to be fulfilled by helping you make your dreams a reality.

Our dreams often contain a kernel of what God has created us to do. You may have a dream of caring for orphans, designing beautiful homes, or becoming a judge. Maybe you had a teacher or counselor who deeply impacted your life, and now you want to be just like her. Those are all worthy dreams that probably have aspects of God's movement in your life. But surrounding the "kernel" of God's call, that dream also has trappings of self that God will ask you to lay down.

> **Our dreams often contain a kernel of what God has created us to do. . . . But surrounding the "kernel" of God's call, that dream also has trappings of self that God will ask you to lay down.**

Jesus said, "Very truly I tell you, unless a kernel of wheat falls to the ground and dies, it remains only a single seed. But if it dies, it produces many seeds."[viii] Without exception, every follower of Jesus Christ is asked to put his or her dreams on the altar of worship with the attitude of "not my will, but yours be done."

Christine shared with me about what this has looked like in her decision to marry Will:

> I prayed intensely, day after day, poring over Scripture with tear-filled eyes, weighing this decision for weeks on end. After a while, I began to notice a theme. The Lord continuously led me back to the Scripture of sacrificing your idols. It was as though He were whispering, "Do you love me enough to lay down your call to the mission field?" What do you mean? I loved the Lord so much I thought going to the mission field was laying down my life. But that's when the stark truth hit. I had made missions my life, my identity, my worth. Missions was filling every bucket intended for the Lord. The truth stung as it settled in. Whether I married Will or not, God was calling me to put this idol on the altar.
>
> A year later, Will and I got married. I wrestled with the sacrifice of Africa every day that year and even for years after. The climactic event in my husband's work each year is a conference for global missions. Every year, I would watch thousands place their prayer cards of commitment on a map as I would sit there and weep. I still desperately wanted that call and some days I still do, but slowly and surely, God is teaching me it's not so much about where or how He's using me, it's about His glory. I am convinced that in His perfect grace, He ordains "sacrifice" as His most precious gift. It teaches us worth in Him we see no other way.

While my life now looks a whole lot like the life I swore I would never live—in the suburbs of middle-class America with three kids and a dog—it is being lived for Him. For some people, laying down your life looks like moving to the slums of a developing country, for me it looks like laying down that call and staying here. We'll never really know until heaven, but I believe the Lord is using Will and my life together for greater kingdom impact than had I gone to the mission field as planned. It doesn't look daunting, sexy, or radical. It looks like a simple daily life of obedience. But through the mundane God is teaching me; He alone is my greatest treasure and my most worthy pursuit.

Sometimes God gives our dreams back to us, and other times He transforms our desires.

You probably aren't in public ministry or hoping to serve in Africa. God has given you a different kernel of a dream than He gave Christine or me, but the same principle applies. Even good things must be continually surrendered to the greatness of knowing Christ Jesus our Lord. It's up to the sovereignty of God if, when, and how He returns them to us.

Becoming True Teammates

Did you know that my husband, Mike, helped me write this book? Actually, he didn't write a word of it and probably won't read it (but he will listen to it on Audible!). He still helped me write this book and every other book I've written. How? Because we are teammates.

As I write these words, I'm staying at a lake house that some friends, Keith and Anna, let us use. But I'm staying alone! Why?

Because my husband knows I need quiet time to think, pray, and write. So, Mike stayed back with our sons to give me this space.

Early in marriage, there is usually a lot of tension around who will do what. You may both have careers and passions that seem to compete. I distinctly remember the seasons of our marriage when we were figuring out who would pick up a sick kid at school when we both had work and whether or not we would move for a job opportunity. In many marriages, these conversations become a tug-of-war, "It's your turn to sacrifice for me!"

Marriage is not ultimately about whose job is more important, but about two people learning to yield to each other out of love. This may mean saying no to exciting opportunities or staying in a job that is less than satisfying. At one point, we moved to Colorado Springs for me to pursue a ministry opportunity even though it put stress on Mike's career. I was really hesitant to make this decision, but Mike believed it was the right thing for us to do. As we prayed, we believed together that we were moving, not for my career, but to be obedient to God.

The most beautiful marriages are formed over years of this type of learning to yield. It's easy to say, "I want to serve God with my life," but the daily interchange of marriage fleshes out our selfishness and stubbornness through the practical decisions of where we live, where we work, and what we do with our time and money. I'm sure you're seeing the pattern throughout all these chapters. God is always working on our character. The issues we are focused on might be finances, sex, in-laws, or career, but the issue God is focused on

> It's easy to say, "I want to serve God with my life," but the daily interchange of marriage fleshes out our selfishness and stubbornness through the practical decisions of where we live, where we work, and what we do with our time and money.

is "Do you love me with all your heart, mind, soul, and strength? Are you following your will or my will?"

You and your husband become the truest of teammates when, together, you want what God wants. This doesn't mean you will agree on everything, but you will agree on the most important thing: "Do not love the world or anything in the world. If anyone loves the world, the love of the Father is not in him. For all that is in the world—the desires of the flesh, the desires of the eyes, and the pride of life—is not from the Father but from the world. The world is passing away, along with its desires; but whoever does the will of God remains forever."[ix]

Endnotes

 i Matthew 22:36–40.

 ii Colossians 3:23 (emphasis added).

 iii Genesis 1:28.

 iv Matthew 28:16–20.

 v Kevin DeYoung, *Just Do Something*. Moody Publishers, 2009), 61.

 vi https://www.ncbi.nlm.nih.gov/pmc/articles/PMC6398854/.

 vii Matthew 8:36.

 viii John 12:24.

 ix I John 2:7.

Chapter 12

the end of the story

One of the most compelling marriage books I have ever read is Linda Dillow's *What's It Like to Be Married to Me?* Linda begins her book in quite an unexpected way. She asks you to picture yourself walking into a funeral. You look around and notice that you know all the people in attendance. Someone hands you a program. As you glance at it, you are shocked to discover that this crowd has gathered to remember your life. This is your memorial service. The keynote speaker is your husband. Linda then asks the reader to ponder the question, "What would your husband say about you?"[i]

I think Solomon would like Linda's opening. He once wrote, "It is better to go to a house of mourning than to go to a house of feasting, for death is the destiny of every man; the living should take this to heart."[ii]

The fact is, you won't be at your own funeral. You will not be able to hear the good or bad things your husband may say about you either in front of a gathered crowd or to his closest confidants. When Solomon encouraged us to take our destiny to heart, I think he was hinting beyond our funeral and even our earthly legacy. One day, you and I will stand before our true husband, Jesus Christ.

As I look over fifty years in the rearview mirror, the reality of my own mortality is sinking in. With the years winding down, I'm not concerned about squeezing in more fun, adventures, and experiences. I'm not the bucket-list type. (That's where my fun husband helps balance me out!) But I am becoming more and more intentional about living my life here in a way that invests in eternal things.

Here's a news flash. Jesus said in response to a question from religious leaders that marriage is not eternal.[iii] Remember when I said that marriage is a metaphor or a form of revelation—that points to God's covenant with his people? Well, the metaphor of marriage will no longer be needed when we experience the unity of being with God in heaven.

Imagine that you want to take your kids to Walt Disney World. You are trying to get them excited about this big trip, so you start showing them videos of what they will experience. You show them Mickey and Donald, Cinderella's castle, and all the fun rides at the theme parks. Your kids watch the videos over and over again.

Once you are actually at Disney, are you going to show your kids those videos? Of course not. They are actually experiencing the reality of *being there*! The promo videos are not needed anymore.

Think of your marriage this way. God created romance, the covenant of marriage, and sex as a promo video to give you a glimpse and to awaken longings for intimacy that were meant to be fulfilled in Him. You were not primarily made for marriage, for sex, or for romance. You were created for intimacy.

> Your marriage is very important to God, but not as important as what He is preparing you for.

Your marriage is very important to God, but not as important as what He is preparing you for.

I didn't write this book primarily to help your marriage. Don't get me wrong. I hope and pray that you have already seen a lot of positive changes between you and your husband. But here's the thing: you will not take your marriage with you to heaven.

Marriage is a wonderful and sacred human relationship, but it is also a temporal one. And so, while I care deeply about your marriage, I care even more about you, about your faith, and about your relationship with God.

It is possible you've read this entire book and taken the message to heart but that you still feel quite hopeless about intimacy in your marriage. Maybe you are like Stephanie.

"I just want to be in love with my husband. Is that too much to ask?" After fourteen years of ups and downs, she was fed up with her self-absorbed, fickle, unheroic man. Although he was not abusive or unfaithful, her husband was insensitive and more concerned about his hobbies and career than improving his relationship with Stephanie. After we met a few times, she told me, "I don't think there is much you can do for me. I will just have to wait it out until I can't take it anymore."

Restoring a marriage is not always about trying harder, being enlightened, or waiting out the tough times. There are some marriages that are just stuck.

Throughout this book, the central theme has been Proverbs 14:1. "The wise woman builds her house, but with her own hands the foolish one tears hers down." Wisdom and effort are essential ingredients to building a solid marriage, but they can't guarantee an intimate relationship. I've seen both men and women do their part to love well, only to be stiff-armed by a spouse who won't respond in kind.

If marriage is ultimately about getting our own needs met, then marriage is over when intimacy fails. Marriage can also be embraced as a relationship that transcends getting our needs met. In some cases, it is the ultimate test of our values and character. Like no other relationship, marriage can highlight our fears and selfishness. The way we respond, especially through disappointment, challenges our core beliefs and our very reason for living.

There are definitely marriages that cannot nor should not continue. The Bible mentions sexual infidelity and a spouse who walks out as examples of when the covenant promise of marriage has been so broken that it might not be repaired.[iv] But Jesus said that marriages ultimately end because of hard hearts.[v] One person is unwilling to confess sin, to forgive, to be honest, or to care. You cannot control your husband's heart, but you are accountable for the state of your own. This is where I want to ask you a question. Are you willing to become a woman of faith?

Becoming a Woman of Faith

Hebrews 11 is known as the hall of fame of faith. It's like a museum of very imperfect men and women who lived their lives with the hope of something they couldn't see. God calls you and me to be such people of faith. "Without faith, it is impossible to please God, because anyone who comes to Him must believe that He exists and that He rewards those who earnestly seek Him."[vi]

Regardless of the state of your marriage, I ask you to reflect on the state of your faith. The writer of Hebrews tells us how to walk by faith, "Keep your eyes fixed on Jesus, the author and perfecter of your faith."[vii] Are you able to look past what's happening in this moment and get a glimpse of God? Can you trust that He is working even if you see no improvement in your husband?

Who do you think of when you picture a modern-day person of faith? Maybe a missionary who knowingly walked into martyrdom or a fearless man or woman who lovingly walked against the tides of culture. Yes, there are stories of great Christians who endured pain and hardship for the sake of their belief in Jesus Christ. But have you ever considered that each one of us is called to live that way, putting our own desires and ambitions aside? Romans 12:1 says that we are to be living sacrifices. Jesus said to His disciples, "If anyone would come after me, he must deny himself and take up his cross and follow me. For whoever wants to save his life will lose it, but whoever loses his life for me will find it."[viii]

You may be willing to die for Christ, but are you willing to live for Him? Are you willing to surrender your longings and depend upon Him? This is a very unpopular question to ask. Our entire culture is built around marriage as a way to fulfill our personal needs and desires. To deny ourselves and willfully stay in a situation that is uncomfortable and unsatisfying is absurd by today's standards. Even many Christian resources will encourage you to leave a marriage if you are not personally fulfilled, but you will not find that advice anywhere in the Bible.

I want to invite you to look past your marriage, with all the ups and downs, and consider who God is forming you into for eternity.

But What About My Needs?

Although God may ask you to persevere through seasons of marriage that are disappointing and unfulfilling, your needs are important to Him. He does not ask you to ignore your longing for love and companionship, but to trust Him with them. In Matthew 6:26 (NIV), Jesus said, "Look at the birds of the air, they do not sow or reap or store away in barns, and yet your heavenly Father feeds them. Are you not much more valuable than they?" Psalm

146:3 (NIV) says, "Do not trust in princes, in mortal men who cannot save." Even the best husband cannot provide salvation—spiritually or emotionally. No matter how good your marriage, you will go through times of drought. Your husband was never meant to completely satisfy you, nor you him.

Perhaps the most touching conversation Jesus had with a human while on Earth was with the Samaritan woman recorded in John 4. This woman had been married five times and was currently living with someone to whom she was not married. She was thirsty for love. Try as she might, the affection of a man never satisfied her. She probably hoped that the next guy just might be the hero she was longing for. Jesus knew her thirst for love, just as he knows yours. He said to her: "Everyone who drinks of this water will be thirsty again, but whoever drinks the water I give him will never thirst. Indeed, the water I give him will become in him a spring of water welling up to eternal life" (John 4:13).[ix]

Is your well dry? Do you feel as if you have little to give your husband? How can you love him when he has given you nothing? Imagine a well of love springing up inside you. No longer are you dependent on your husband's touch or compliment to make it through the day. He, beloved, is your Bridegroom. Only He is able to love you perfectly. He loves you with "an everlasting love." None of us deserves God's love and mercy. It has nothing to do with our merit or love for Him. He simply loves us! No matter what has transpired in your past, Jesus is asking to be your loving husband.

Please do not allow either your disappointment or your happiness in marriage to interfere with what is most important—intimacy with God. Both the excitement of a growing marriage and the despair of brokenness are chances to seek and glorify the Lord. What an inspiration the apostle Paul was in his letter to the

Philippians when he wrote, "I know what it is to be in need, and I know what it is to have plenty. I have learned the secret of being content in any and every situation....I can do everything through him who gives me strength."ˣ

From an eternal perspective, our marriages are not an end in and of themselves. They are the vehicle through which God can refine us and teach us love. God wants to be glorified through you in your marriage: for better or worse, for richer or poorer, in sickness and in health, till death separates you. This is not a pessimistic message! It means wherever you are, God can restore and redeem you. He may not "fix" your marriage—that takes two willing people. But He can and will make you into a beautiful representation of Him if you are surrendered to Him. Nothing can interfere with your faithfulness to God except your will to resist Him.

While I've been honored to meet some high-profile Christian leaders who do great things for God, the greatest faith I've witnessed in my life has been knowing men and women who steadily obey God, loving through hardship. These people are not weak. They confront sin and injustice, but they do so with a humble and steadfast confidence that there is more to this life than what we can see today. Faith means staking your life on the eternal.

One day my marriage will end. Mike and I will be separated by death, and we will each enter eternity. I will thank God for the good gifts He gave me in marriage, but more importantly, I will offer to God my faithfulness. I want to live for *that* day. When those who know me best reflect on my life, let them not say, "She was a happy wife," but "She was a faithful woman." May the same be said of you!

Faith means staking your life on the eternal.

Endnotes

   i Linda Dillow, *What's It Like to Be Married to Me?* David C. Cook, 2001), 29–30.

  ii Ecclesiastes 7:2.

 iii Matthew 22:30.

 iv See I Corinthians 7:14–15, Matthew 5:31–32, and Matthew 19:9.

  v Matthew 19:8.

 vi Hebrews 11:6.

vii Hebrews 12:2.

viii Matthew 16:24–25.

 ix John 4:13.

  x Philippians 4:12–13.

study guide

How to Use This Guide

My bookshelves are lined with books I've found helpful, but learning and actually applying what we have learned are two different things. Without taking time to reflect and digest, we can quickly forget what God is showing us.

This study guide is designed to make what you've read sticky. You might find encouragement, accountability, and a place to talk through the content by going through this book in a small group setting. Questions from this guide can help direct your conversation. You might also find this study guide helpful for your own personal reflection or devotional time with God.

You will see that for each week, the guide is broken down into three sections.

What Do You Think? has questions that help you begin to apply what you have just read to your real-life marriage. Those questions are great journal prompts or discussion starters in a group setting. *Digging for Wisdom* will get you into God's Word. Ultimately, you don't want to learn from me but from God Himself! Each week, the *Making It Real* section provides a challenge that will help you put into practice what you are learning.

Chapter 1
Disappointment: The End or Beginning of Intimacy?

What Do You Think?

1. Try to remember back to your wedding day. What hopes and expectations did you have for your marriage? Were they realistic?
2. How has your disappointment impacted your desire to be intimate with your husband?
3. Do you think intimacy in marriage comes easily to anyone? Why or why not?
4. Why do you think God created women with desires for intimacy that will never be fully achieved in marriage?
5. Do you think every husband has a hero within? Why or why not?
6. What do you think it means to find the hero in your husband?

Digging for Wisdom

1. Read Proverbs 14:1. What does wisdom have to do with the state of your marriage? What does this verse say about your power as a wife?
2. Read Proverbs 1:20–32. How does wisdom cry out to you? What will happen if you continually ignore her pleas? What wisdom do you find difficult to accept as a wife?
3. If your fairy tale is in a state of despair, can God still give you wisdom? Read James 1:2–8. What are the criteria for receiving wisdom from God?
4. Read Proverbs 4:7–9, 8:34, 9:10, and 19:20. How can a foolish woman become wise?

Making It Real

Write a letter or prayer to God about your marriage. Talk to Him about your disappointments and your fears. Ask Him for the wisdom to "build your house."

Chapter 2
Power for a Purpose

What Do You Think?

1. How do you think your husband's needs translate into your power?
2. What did you learn about your husband's need for respect?
3. In what ways do you see your husband's fear of failure impacting your marriage?
4. What do you think it looks like to be your husband's helper? Give some specific examples.
5. What is the difference between meeting your husband's sexual needs and sharing your husband's sexual journey?

Digging for Wisdom

1. Read Matthew 25:14–30. This passage is often used to teach about investing our money and abilities, but it can be applied to everything God has given us to steward. What does this passage say about how you steward or invest the power God has given you in your marriage?
2. Look up these passages that use the word *ezer*. What does each passage teach you about what this means to be a helper in your marriage and for God to be your helper?
   Genesis 2:18–20
   Exodus 18:4
   Deuteronomy 33:26
   Psalm 33:20
   Psalm 121:1–2
3. Proverbs 31:10–12. How is this godly wife described in these verses? How does she use her power?
4. David prayed, "Search me, O God, and know my heart." Ask God

to search your heart and show you how you are using the power
He has given you within your marriage. Write your response here:

_____

_____

_____

Making It Real

Ask your husband how you are doing in these three areas: respecting
him, being a teammate, and sharing his sexual journey. Ask him to
give you specific ways that you can improve the use of your power in
these three areas.

Chapter 3
Nobody Told Me That Marriage Could Be So Lonely

What Do You Think?

1. Why are intimacy and self-protection incompatible? (Read I John 4:18.)
2. Why are many men more hesitant than women when it comes to pursuing intimacy?
3. How might a husband's need for intimacy differ from his wife's need for intimacy?
4. What are your two greatest emotional needs as a wife? To what extent are these needs currently being met? How might your fear discourage you from seeking intimacy with your husband?
5. What are your husband's greatest emotional needs in marriage? To what extent are you meeting these needs? How might his feelings of vulnerability discourage him from seeking intimacy with you?

Digging for Wisdom

1. Read Colossians 3:1–18. If you are a believer in Christ, how does God call you to relate toward your husband? How is he called to behave toward you? How will these instructions demonstrate Christlike love and pave the way for intimacy?
2. Read I Corinthians 13:4–7, James 1:19–20, and Ephesians 4:26–32. How do anger, selfishness, and bitterness interfere with God's design for unity?
3. Read Psalm 139. Remember that "The word *intimate* comes from a Latin word that means 'innermost.' It's the idea of knowing someone in their innermost self and embracing them completely." What does this Psalm say about the level of God's intimacy with you? Based on

this Psalm, how would you describe David's intimacy with the Lord?

4. How did David's intimacy with God help him weather disappointment and betrayal from close friends and family?

5. Why is intimacy with God so vital to pursuing intimacy with your husband?

Making It Real

God says, "Draw near to me and I will draw near to you" and "You will find me when you seek me with your whole heart." What steps do you need to take to draw near to God? Here are a few suggestions:

- Pour out your heart to God. Tell Him about your disappointment and fears.
- Ask for God to give you the wisdom and strength to change how you view your husband and marriage.
- Spend some time each day reading and meditating on Psalms. Journal about what you learn about God.
- Show your husband the cycles of intimacy and self-protection. Together talk about a time when you were on each of these cycles. What is one thing you can do together to take a step toward intimacy?

Chapter 4
God Works in Mysterious Ways

What Do You Think?

1. What is your gut reaction to the word *submission*?
2. What surprised you or challenged you in this chapter?
3. What do you think is the difference between having a quiet and gentle spirit versus being a quiet, passive person?
4. Do you agree with the statement that biblical submission promotes intimacy in marriage? Why or why not?
5. In your own words, what does it mean for you to submit to your husband? On a scale from one to ten, how willing are you to do this?

Digging for Wisdom

1. Read Ephesians 5:22 and Colossians 3:18. What do the phrases, "as to the Lord" and "as is fitting to the Lord" mean related to the command for a wife to submit to her husband?
2. Read Genesis 3:16. How does this verse echo the frustrations you feel as a wife? Describe the tensions between wanting to be led by your husband but wanting to control him at the same time.
3. Read I Corinthians 1:18–31 and James 3:13–18. Our culture tells us that a wife's submission in marriage is an archaic and foolish concept. What does the Bible say about the world's wisdom compared to God's design?

Making It Real

Look for three opportunities this week to choose to have a submissive heart toward your husband.

Chapter 5
A Time to Stand Up

What Do You Think?

1. Why is it so critical to understand that submitting to a husband is ultimately about submitting to the Lord?

2. What are the three reasons given for why a wife should stand up to her husband? Think of times when one of these circumstances has arisen in your marriage. How did you handle it?

3. Why is standing up at the appropriate time an essential aspect of finding the hero in your husband?

4. Describe the difference between empowering and enabling your husband.

5. What is the difference between taking responsibility for your husband's choices and influencing his choices? Give practical examples.

Digging for Wisdom

1. Read Romans 13:1, 1 Peter 2:13, and Acts 5:27–29. What do these verses teach about the importance and limits of submission?

2. Read Psalm 141:4–5, Proverbs 27:5–6, Ecclesiastes 4:9–10, 2 Thessalonians 3:14–15, and Luke 6:41–42. What do these verses teach about enabling others in sin?

3. Read Matthew 7:1–5 and Galatians 6:1–5. What do these passages say about the importance of having the right heart when we confront?

4. Read 1 Samuel 25.
   - How is Abigail described in this passage?
   - How is Nabal described in this passage?
   - Would you describe Abigail as a submissive wife? Why or why not?
   - What do you learn about a wise wife's role in this passage?

Making It Real

Choose an issue in your marriage on which you believe it is important to take a stand. Now develop a plan based on these three steps:

1. Check your heart. Ask the Lord to search your heart and to show you if there is anything you need to confess and address in your attitude toward your husband.

2. Get help. List resources (people, podcasts, books, or other resources) that can help you confront this situation wisely. What steps do you need to take to get support and wisdom?

3. State the problem and let God fight for you. Write a letter (you may decide to have a conversation with your husband rather than giving him a letter, but this will help you get your thoughts together) stating the issue, what you resolve to do on your part, and an invitation for your husband to also address what's happening. Then put the issue before the Lord in prayer.

Chapter 6
A Wife's Greatest Dilemma

What Do You Think?

1. In your own words, describe a wife's greatest dilemma. How has this played out in your marriage?
2. What weaknesses in your husband make you want to take over? How are these weaknesses the flip side of his strengths?
3. Go back and review the different ways that women take over. Write down the ones that best describe you.
4. Share an example of when you have used this strategy to overpower your husband. What were you afraid of? How did it play out?
5. How do you think you could have handled the situation by using your power to build up rather than tear down.
6. How does this situation reveal *your* immaturity? How is God asking you to grow in this area?

Digging for Wisdom

1. Read Genesis 3:1–19. How do you see "a wife's greatest dilemma" played out in this passage? What insight does this passage give you into your marriage?
2. Read Galatians 5:16–26. How does Paul describe spiritual immaturity and immaturity in this passage? How does this list give you new eyes to see your own immaturity rather than focusing on how your husband needs to grow up?
3. Read Psalm 46, 62:5–10, 118:8–9, 146: and Matthew 6:25–34. What does each of these passages say about trusting God when you can't trust men?
4. Read Hebrews 11:1–12:3 and Romans 8:5–17. How is submission exercising faith in God—trusting what you can't see? Why is it so important to your walk with the Lord?

Making It Real

Look at the list of the five practical steps you can take to resign as the boss. Write down here how you implemented at least two of these steps in real life scenarios in your marriage this week.

Chapter 7
Your Last Fight

What Do You Think?

1. How would you describe the difference between a fight and a conflict?
2. When did you and your husband have a conflict that didn't end up in a fight?
3. How do you usually "dress" for conflict? How do these fighting clothes create a fight rather than a healthy conflict?
4. What do you think about the research suggesting that two-thirds of marital conflict is unresolvable?
5. Which of the seven steps to addressing conflict is most difficult for you and why?
6. Think of a time when you ignored conflict. How did that affect your marriage? Why is it important to address conflict rather than ignoring it?

Digging for Wisdom

1. Read John 17:20–23. Who is Jesus praying for in this passage? What does He pray for them?
2. Read Matthew 5:46–48. How are Christians called to love uniquely? How does this apply to loving your husband through conflict?
3. Read Ephesians 4:17–32. If you read this passage before conflict with your husband, how might your heart be different?
4. What do you think Paul meant when he wrote, "Do not grieve the Holy Spirit?" How have you grieved the Holy Spirit in conflict?

Making It Real

If your husband is willing, read together through the seven steps of healthy conflict. Discuss which one is most difficult for you as a couple.

Chapter 8
How Did We Get Here?

What Do You Think?

1. What did you learn about the role of a wife from your mother? What did you learn about the role of a husband from your father? How have those lessons affected your marriage, for better or for worse?

2. How have earlier experiences in your life affected how you view God? What truths about God do you struggle to accept as a result? What truths about yourself do you struggle to accept?

3. What are the current cultural expectations of marriage both within the church and in secular society? How are these expectations different from God's design for marriage?

4. Describe a time when you tried to fight sin with determination and self-control. What happened? How would it be different to address this sin through surrender? What would it require for you to surrender?

5. To what extent are the difficulties in your marriage due to an *unwillingness* to change rather than an *inability* to change?

Digging for Wisdom

1. Read Galatians 5:19–21, Romans 1:29–32, II Timothy 3:2–5, and Proverbs 6:16–19. Anger, sexual immorality, drunkenness—these are obvious sins that often destroy marriages. What are the subtler sins listed along with the obvious ones? How do these subtle sins destroy intimacy in marriage?

2. Read Romans 7:18–24. Even when we desire to do what is right, we are naturally drawn towards sin. What sinful desires do you have that compel you to "wage war against" in your marriage? What can you do about this (read Psalm 139:23–24 and Psalm 51)?

3. Read Romans 8. What did the discouraged Paul from Romans 7 discover in order to write the encouragement recorded in Romans 8:31–39?

Making It Real

Have a conversation this week with your husband about how either your childhood experiences or your expectations for marriage have impacted you. (Some of the "what do you think?" questions might be good conversation starters.)

Chapter 9
Learning to Make Love

What Do You Think?

1. What did you expect sex in marriage to be like when you first got married? Did the reality match your expectations? If so, how?

2. What do you honestly think of this statement: "It should actually feel unnatural to think about sex *apart from thinking about God*"? Why is there so often a disconnect between how we think about sex and God?

3. Why is understanding marriage as a covenant so important to having the right perspective on your sex life?

4. How is God teaching you to love through the challenges of sex in your marriage?

5. What obstacles have you and your husband faced on your journey of sexual intimacy? How has God used these obstacles to draw you into deeper intimacy?

6. What do you think it looks like to sexually "play offense" in this season of your marriage?

Digging for Wisdom

1. Read Revelation 19:9 and 22:17. Why do you think God uses the imagery of a wedding to describe our impending union with Christ?

2. Read Ezekiel 16:1–29. In this disturbing passage, God uses vivid sexual language to describe Israel's infidelity. Why do you think God uses the metaphor of sexual covenant in this way?

3. Read Proverbs 5:1–20. How does this father encourage his son to play both defense and offense related to sexual desire?

4. Read Song of Solomon 7:11–18 (feel free to read the whole book if you have time!). What does this passage tell you about God's view of marital sexual love?

Making it Real

Pick one of the three suggestions under playing offense to work on this week. Write down how you will 1. Learn to say yes; 2. Make time for sex; or 3. Let go of perfection.

Chapter 10
Your Hero in Your Home

What Do You Think?

1. On a scale from 1 to 10, how "safe" do you think your home is for your husband emotionally? Explain your answer.
2. Which of the four areas discussed (household responsibilities, money, in-laws, and parenting) do you think represents the greatest area of potential defeat for your husband?
3. Why is it important to have a healthy perspective of both unity and your personal autonomy in marriage?
4. How are you and your husband doing in the journey of "leaving" your father and mother? Why is leaving so critical to cleaving?
5. Why is living in God's grace so critical to "finding the hero in your husband?"

Digging for Wisdom

1. Read Philippians 2:1–4. (Yes, I know we've read these verses before!) Imagine that you and your husband are in marriage counseling and Paul is your counselor. These verses are the advice that he gives you about one of the four categories from question 2 above. How would you apply it?
2. Genesis 28–31 records the story of Jacob and his wives, Rachel and Leah. If you're unfamiliar with the story, you may want to check it out. How did "in-laws," even thousands of years ago, interfere with God's design for marriage?
3. We have another story of a father-in-law in Exodus 18. How was Moses' father-in-law a blessing to him? Contrast Laban's and Jethro's influence.
4. Read Hebrews 4:15–16. What encouragement does this verse give you about your weaknesses and failures?

Making It Real

Based on what you read in this chapter, what is one step you need to take this week to make your home an encouraging and welcoming place for your husband?

Chapter 11
Work: His, Mine, and Ours

What Do You Think?

1. Do you think your and your husband's work matter to God? Why or why not? Have you ever thought of your work as an overflow of your personhood? How so?
2. Describe why work may have a different significance in your husband's life than it does in yours.
3. What are specific ways you can encourage your husband's character through his work rather than focusing only on his achievements or paycheck?
4. Describe the "season" in which you and your husband are currently. What does work look like for each of you in this season?
5. In what ways do you identify with Christine's story? What has God asked you to surrender in this season?
6. What would it look like for you and your husband to be teammates in your approach to work?

Digging for Wisdom

How do each of the following verses challenge your approach to work:

Colossians 3:23–24
I Corinthians 15:58
Matthew 6:25–34
II Timothy 3:16–17
John 14:12
Titus 2:9–10
Luke 16:10

Read Psalm 47:4, Matthew 6:33, 10:38–39, and Philippians 3:7–14. What do these verses teach us about our dreams and passions? Does God ever ask us to give up our dreams?

Making It Real

Ask your husband, "What is one way I can be more supportive of your work life or career?" or "How can I be more sensitive to the pressures you face around work?"

Chapter 12
The End of the Story

What Do You Think?

1. "Your marriage is very important, but not as important as what it is preparing for." What do you think of this statement? How does it challenge your perspective of marriage?
2. Why is walking by faith essential to finding the hero in your husband?
3. How can you see God preparing you for eternity, working on your character, and teaching you about intimacy with Him through your marriage?

Digging for Wisdom

1. Read Hebrews 11. How would you describe a modern-day woman who lives by faith? Why is earthly disappointment and loss an essential part of developing faith in God?
2. Read Hebrews 12:1–13. List at least seven specific things this passage tells us to do if we want to become like the "faith heroes" in Hebrews 11.
3. What is God asking you to practically do based on what you read in Hebrews?

Making It Real

Write your own version of a "by faith" statement. For example, "By faith, Jannelle endured through years of disappointment with her eyes fixed on Jesus, trusting Him to give her the wisdom and strength to love Mark."

resources

Finding a Christian counselor:

focusonthefamily.com/get-help/counseling-services-and-referrals/

Sexual addiction:

Find a counselor: *iitap.com*

Find a group: *PureDesire.org*

Husband addicted to porn: *fightforloveministries.org*

Sexual abuse recovery:

The Wounded Heart: Hope for Adult Victims of Childhood Sexual Abuse by Dan Allender

On the Threshold of Hope: Opening the Door to Healing for Survivors of Sexual Abuse by Diane Mandt Langberg, PhD

Sexual disorders:

Mycounselor.online

In a potentially destructive marriage:

Domestic violence help: *thehotline.org/*

The Emotionally Destructive Marriage: How to Find Your Voice and Reclaim Your Hope by Leslie Vernick

Recovering from infidelity:

Torn Asunder: Recovering from an Extramarial Affair by Dave Carder

relationalcare.org/intensive-retreats

Great books on marriage and relationships:

What's It Like to be Married to Me? And Other Dangerous Questions by Linda Dillow

Boundaries: When to Say YES, When to Say NO, to Take Control of Your Life by Henry Cloud and John Townsend

Vertical Marriage: The One Secret That Will Change Your Marriage by Dave and Ann Wilson

How We Love: Discover Your Love Style, Enhance Your Marriage by Milo and Kay Yerkovich

Fight Your Way to a Better Marriage: How Healthy Conflict Can Take You to Deeper Levels of Intimacy by Dr. Greg Smalley

The Meaning of Marriage: Facing the Complexities of Commitment with the Wisdom of God by Timothy Keller with Kathy Keller

Books on sexual intimacy:

A Celebration of Sex: A Guide to Enjoying God's Gift of Sexual Intimacy by Dr. Douglas E. Roseneau

Our Bodies Tell God's Story: Discovering the Divine Plan for Love, Sex, and Gender by Christopher West

Juli's books and ministry:

Authenticintimacy.com

Java with Juli podcast

Passion Pursuit: What Kind of Love Are You Making?

Surprised by the Healer: Embracing Hope for Your Broken Story

Rethinking Sexuality: God's Design and Why It Matters

God, Sex and Your Marriage